LIVING STUDIES

is a series of high quality Christian books, both timely and relevant to today's problems and challenges. □ In addition to being some of the best in Christian reading, books in the LIVING STUDIES SERIES have a dual purpose, being specially designed for small group Bible studies, midweek services, adult vacation Bible school, or as adult Sunday school elective studies. □ A separate Leader's Guide, designed for easy out-of-class preparation, makes any lay person into an interesting and capable discussion leader. Books and Leader's Guides (some for six sessions, most for thirteen sessions) are available at your Christian bookstore or write Tyndale House Publishers, Box 80, Wheaton IL 60189.

LEADERSHIP LIFESTYLE

AJITH FERNANDO

LIVING STUDIES
Tyndale House Publishers, Inc.,
Wheaton, Illinois

To George E. Good, Sam Sherrard,
Robert E. Coleman, and Daniel P. Fuller,
with gratitude to God for their investment
in my life.

Much of the material in chapter one is taken from
the author's talk "The Ministry of Multiplication,"
which was first given at the International
Conference for Itinerant Evangelists in
Amsterdam, The Netherlands, in July 1983.
It is published in *The Work of an Evangelist,*
© 1984 World Wide Publications. All rights
reserved. Used by permission.

Unless otherwise noted, all Scriptures are from the
Holy Bible, New International Version © 1978 by
New York International Bible Society

First printing, September 1985
Library of Congress Catalog Card Number 85-50952
ISBN 0-8423-2130-6
Copyright © 1985 by Ajith Fernando
All rights reserved
Printed in the United States of America

CONTENTS

FOREWORD

Leadership is always crucial to the church's worldwide enterprise. But at the present moment, it seems to me leadership is especially urgent.

In the West, the generation of post-World War II leaders has begun and led outstanding movements of evangelism, missions, education, lay ministries, and social concern. Within the next decade, many of these "giants" will need to pass on the mantle to others.

In the so-called Two-Thirds world, older leaders must harness the energies of younger men and women to disciple vast numbers of new converts, develop churches, and evangelize huge numbers of unreached peoples.

Every leader should be asking: "Who is going to take my place? Who is God raising up? How can I help encourage the coming leaders?"

In looking for leaders, we must look for more than personalities. God does not look on outward appearances. Nor should we be seeking only "organization men and women" who can keep machinery going. Without vision the machinery will rust, perish, and produce to no avail.

We need godly leaders who are spiritually prepared, biblically grounded, and practically alert. For these reasons, I welcome Ajith Fernando's *Leadership Life-Style*.

It is well based on a masterpiece of leadership training. Paul's letter to Timothy is God's inspired gift to us. Paul shows how leaders should be sought, taught, encouraged, warned, and directed.

Also, it is well written. The author has thought clearly, read widely, and written practically.

Equally important, it is well lived! Ajith Fernando is one of the outstanding younger leaders I have met. I have seen his own earnest desire to seek advice about how he can grow in his work. I have seen how he respects older leaders, but is not afraid tactfully to disagree. In Sri Lanka, he has adopted the Youth For Christ staff which he directs as his own "Timothys."

I pray that *Leadership Life-Style* will be widely used, not only because it is a good book, but because it comes from a man whose life is a living demonstration.

Leighton Ford, Evangelist
Charlotte, North Carolina

FOREWORD

No title could be more appropriate than *Leadership Life-Style* for a book written by Ajith Fernando. Ajith is the kind of man who practices what he preaches. And this book is a practical exposure of that process, the same one used by Paul with his disciple Timothy.

Ajith Fernando came to the United States from Sri Lanka to study and indeed gained a great deal from his experience in the West. However, he didn't become a carbon copy of Western Christians but has maintained his integrity as an Asian and as a result gives back to us much more than he took when he came here for his graduate education.

I feel that reading Ajith's writings is a kind of return to the mental process that typified the Jewish mind of Jesus' day and helps us to see beyond the Greek and Western influences that have so affected our way of thinking. This is a rich and instructive book that I believe will become a standard teaching tool on discipleship and a valuable aid and study of 1 Timothy.

Jay Kesler, President
Youth For Christ,
Wheaton, Illinois

PREFACE

This study of 1 Timothy is the result of a request from some of my colleagues in Youth For Christ to prepare a study on disciple making. Since I am committed to the Bible as the basic textbook for such training, I decided to use 1 and 2 Timothy as a basis for these studies. In these books we can observe Paul, a great disciple maker, equipping his spiritual child Timothy. The treasures contained in 1 Timothy proved to be so vast that I decided to confine the studies on disciple making to that book. To learn how Paul made disciples, I lived in 1 Timothy for more than one and a half years.

As my studies progressed, I decided to broaden the focus somewhat and to study the more general theme of Christian leadership, of which disciple making is a vital part. My approach has been to learn about leadership from two viewpoints, both of which are reflected in this book.

First, we will observe the way the great Christian leader, Paul, exercised his leadership role in his relationship with Timothy. From that example we will glean principles about how to lead. Second, we will study what Paul told the young leader, Timothy, about how he should fulfill his leadership responsibilities. First Timothy is ideally suited for this because it is essentially a book of instructions on leadership.

When working with a text of 1 Timothy, I first studied and meditated on the text personally and noted my observations.

Then I looked at what the great commentators of 1 Timothy had to say about the text. This step sometimes led me to correct my misinterpretations and always enriched my understanding (I am deeply grateful to the church in the West for her great contribution to the church universal in terms of exegetical scholarship). Throughout this process, I kept asking the question, what does this text have to say to Christian leaders? So, one of my chief aims was to apply the principles contained in 1 Timothy to situations a leader faces today.

Most of the fruit of my study and meditation was shared with the members of the Council of Youth For Christ in Colombo, a group of young preachers who minister with YFC on a volunteer or full-time capacity, whom I have the privilege of teaching regularly. These meetings were marked by lively discussions. I had to revise and refine my material quite often because of their pertinent observations and probing questions.

Some of these studies were done with leaders of other Christian organizations both in Sri Lanka and Pakistan. Portions of chapter 1 were given in an address at the Amsterdam '83 Conference for Itinerant Evangelists.

I was finally able to put these studies into their present form when the YFC family permitted me to reduce my responsibilities in YFC for a period so that I could devote more time to writing.

This book is not intended to be a commentary. It harnesses the scholarship of the commentaries and seeks to apply it to the life and ministry of Christian leaders. Many very important passages in 1 Timothy have not been included in our study or only skimmed through because they were considered to be outside the scope of our study.

I have written this book primarily with Christian leaders and prospective leaders in mind. It may be used for personal study or for teaching small groups, or it could be read as a devotional book. The assignments given at the end of the lessons are aimed at helping the reader to apply the truths he has learned to his personal life.

I have dedicated this book to four Christian leaders who have deeply influenced me. The first, my pastor in my teenage years, introduced me to the beauty of godliness. The second, the founding director of Youth For Christ in Sri Lanka, has been to me like what Paul was to Timothy. The other two are seminary teachers who were models of godliness and of careful scholarship, of deep commitment to both evangelism and personal ministry.

I wish to express my gratitude to Mrs. Faith Berman and Mrs. Sakuntala Dayapala, who typed the manuscript of this book, and to my wife, my father, and Mrs. Parames Blacker, who helped in the proofreading.

ONE
LEADERSHIP AS
PARENTHOOD (1:2, 3)

Leadership today is often viewed only in terms of the position and responsibilities one holds in an organization. The higher one is in the framework, the more important a leader he is thought to be. Certainly this is an important aspect of leadership. But when Christians look at leadership, they view it in terms of people rather than position. One of the most beautiful figures used in the Scriptures to describe the relationship the leader has with his people is in terms of parenthood.

Leadership in the Bible is viewed first of all as the influence for good one has on another. A leader's first task is not to keep the machinery of an organization moving and fulfilling its goals but to help those under him to live and serve in obedience to the will of God. It is only in this way that God's goals for the organization can be fulfilled. From the viewpoint of the Scriptures, an organization is like a family, and the leader is like the father of this family.

WHAT SPIRITUAL PARENTHOOD MEANS (1:2)

Paul addressed Timothy as "my true son in the faith." In what sense was Paul Timothy's spiritual father?

First, we are almost sure that Paul was Timothy's spiritual father through evangelism. Timothy was probably converted during Paul's first visit to Lystra. The fact that Paul had been "the human instrument in Timothy's conversion" (Stott, *Guard the Gospel,* InterVarsity, 1973) would certainly qualify him to regard himself as Timothy's father. This gives the first possible use of the parent figure when applied to Christian leadership. A leader may be called a parent because he helped give spiritual birth to a child.

This seems to be the parenthood Paul was talking about in Philemon 10. Paul wrote: "I appeal to you for my son Onesimus, who became my son while I was in chains." Philemon's slave Onesimus had previously been useless to him. But things had changed. He had become "a dear brother" (v. 16). Onesimus had been converted through the ministry of Paul and had thus become a child begotten of Paul.

Second, Paul was Timothy's father through concern and affection. This is implied by the word "son" which Paul used here. Instead of using the more common word, normally translated "son" *(huios,* appearing 380 times in the New Testament), he used a more affectionate word, which is normally translated "child" *(teknon,* appearing 100 times), a word suggesting tenderness and endearment.

In some other instances, when Paul used this word to address his spiritual children, we see the idea of affection and concern emerging more clearly. Paul, writing to the wayward Galatian Christians, said: "My dear children [*tekna*], for whom I am again in the pains of childbirth until Christ is formed in you, how I wish I could be with you now and change my tone, because I am perplexed about you!" (Gal. 4:19, 20). To the Thessalonians he wrote, "We were gentle among you, like a mother caring for her little children [*tekna*]. We loved you so much that we were delighted to share with you not only the gospel of God but our lives as well, because you had become so dear to us" (1 Thess. 2:7, 8). A little later Paul said, "For you know that we dealt with each of you as a father deals with his own children [*tekna*], encouraging, comforting and urging you to live lives worthy of God" (1 Thess. 2:11, 12).

Affection and concern, then, is a second idea conveyed by Paul's use of the parent figure. To be a spiritual parent is to exercise tender loving care toward our children. John Stott in his book, *The Preacher's Portrait* (London: The Tyndale Press, 1961), says that the designation of the preacher as a father is used essentially to describe the preacher's affection and concern for his spiritual family.

The affection and concern Paul felt for Timothy is clearly seen in this epistle. Paul wanted him to achieve God's best for him (1:18). We see his concern for Timothy's physical health (5:23), and his spiritual health (4:12-16; 6:11-16).

Most of this epistle came from a concern for Timothy's ministry, for the letter contains mostly instructions about Timothy's specific responsibilities. Perhaps the most beautiful glimpse of the affection between Paul and Timothy is shown in 2 Timothy 1:3, 4: "I thank God . . . as night and day I constantly remember you in my prayers. Recalling your tears, I long to see you, so that I may be filled with joy."

Third, Paul was Timothy's father through a special discipleship ministry. Paul described Timothy as his "true son," the word "true" meaning "genuine." Paul also used this word of his relationship with Titus (Titus 1:4). Paul seemed to imply from the use of that word that as a genuine child, Timothy was running true to his spiritual parentage, showing a real resemblance to his father.

While Paul seemed to view Christians in the congregations he founded as his children in a general sense, Timothy and Titus were his children in a particular sense. Just after calling the Corinthians his "dear children" (1 Cor. 4:14), Paul said, "I am sending to you Timothy, my son whom I love, who is faithful in the Lord. He will remind you of my way of life in Christ Jesus, which agrees with what I teach everywhere in every church" (1 Cor. 4:17). Paul was saying here that Timothy was his son in a special sense in that he knew exactly how Paul acted and taught. Ralph Martin said that Paul "regarded him as almost an extension of his own personality" *(Colossians and Philemon, New Century Bible Commentary,* Eerdmans, 1973).

Before Paul could have such confidence in Timothy, he first had to invest himself in Timothy. Paul and Timothy had developed a *guru-shishya* relationship. The father-son terminology to express the master-disciple relationship seemed to be widespread in Paul's day. Elisha had this type of relationship with Elijah. So he could call Elijah, "my father" (2 Kings 2:12).

So, from observing Paul's relationship with Timothy and Titus, we can conclude that a spiritual father trains a few of his spiritual children in a particularly detailed and comprehensive manner, spending an extended amount of time with them individually. This certainly was the method of Jesus. Even though he never neglected the masses, he concentrated upon training a few men who took his message to the world.

A leader, therefore, is sometimes called a spiritual parent because he has introduced a person to a saving knowledge of Christ. He is also a spiritual parent to every person he leads because he relates to them with tender loving care. Finally, to a few under his care, he is a spiritual parent in the sense of being a discipler who individually disciples that person to maturity in Christ and trains him or her to be effective in the service of Christ. In the relationship between Paul and Timothy, all three of these aspects of parenthood seem to apply.

WHAT SPIRITUAL PARENTHOOD DOES NOT MEAN

We must hasten to add a caution concerning spiritual parenthood because some have abused the role. Knowing of these abuses, Jesus said, "Do not call anyone on earth 'father,' for you have one Father, and he is in heaven" (Matt. 23:9). Jesus was warning his followers of the pride and hypocrisy of the Pharisees, who loved "the place of honor at banquets and the most important seats in the synagogues; they love to be greeted in the marketplaces, and to have men call them 'Rabbi' " (Matt. 23:6, 7). Such treatment gave them a sense of superiority over other people.

Some people want to be parents because they want the status and glory they think spiritual parenthood brings. They fail to see that such glory belongs to God alone. Jesus clearly said, just before his command not to call anyone on earth "father," "You have only one Master and you are all brothers" (Matt. 23:8).

As far as status is concerned, our spiritual children are on an equal footing with us. We are brothers and sisters under a common Master and Father.

Related to this unhealthy quest for status from spiritual parenthood is what Leroy Eims describes as the "danger of developing a possessive attitude" (*The Lost Art of Disciple Making*, Zondervan, 1978). Eims says that this danger usually manifests itself in the spiritual parent "using terms such as 'My man,' 'My team,' 'My trainees.' " He points out that, "in the New Testament . . . though Paul and the other apostles felt close to the people to whom they ministered and referred to them at times as their 'little children,' they were also quick to remind them that they actually belonged to Jesus Christ."

According to Eims, another way this possessiveness toward disciples shows itself is when the trainer "is hesitant to expose them to other men of God who can have an impact on their lives." He is threatened by these other leaders because "his own ministry might lose some of its luster in the eyes of his men, if they see others who are equally gifted perhaps with strengths and abilities that he does not have."

This possessiveness is alien to the Scriptures. We have no exclusive hold on anybody. A Paul will plant the seed, and an Apollos will water. But it is God who makes it grow (1 Cor. 3:6). God alone has exclusive rights to anybody's life. We take the responsibilities of spiritual parenthood seriously and disciple a person for as long as God wishes us to do so, always remembering that the disciple does not belong to us. So, while he is under our care, we will gladly expose him to anyone from whom he can benefit. And when the time comes, we will release him to the work God has for him.

Second Timothy 1:5 shows that Paul recognized without any hesitation other important influences in the life of Timothy. Paul said, "I have been reminded of your sincere faith, which first lived in your grandmother Lois and in your mother Eunice and, I am persuaded, now lives in you also." Timothy was Paul's spiritual child. But he was also the spiritual child of his mother and grandmother. A discipling ministry can often bring a strain in family relationships. Parents could resent the new influence of this person who suddenly presumes to have taken the place of a parent in their child's life. Such unfortunate misunderstandings could be minimized if the discipler makes a genuine effort to avoid possessiveness.

What we have just said does not imply that the discipler has no authority at all. As the representative of the One who has all authority, he is invested with a derived or secondary authority. He is like a servant who looks after the Master's children. In 2 Corinthians 4:5, Paul called himself the servant of the Corinthian Christians. A servant is not a bigwig, but when the children go astray, the servant (or nanny) may need to discipline the children.

So Paul, after telling the Corinthians, "I became your father through the gospel" (1 Cor. 4:15), went on to say that he may have to exercise discipline the next time he comes to Corinth. He asked, "Shall I come to you with a whip, or in love and with a gentle spirit?" (v. 21). As a spiritual father, Paul could have come both as a disciplinarian and as a gentle encourager. Yet all of his authority as a spiritual parent was derived from God, whose servant he was. In the ultimate sense, God alone is the spiritual father.

SETTLING CHILDREN IN MINISTRY (1:3)

One of the most important things Paul did to his spiritual child, Timothy, was to train and settle him in the ministry. This is evident in 1:3 where Paul said, "As I urged you when I went into Macedonia, stay there in Ephesus so that you may command certain men not to teach false doctrine."

Timothy's Assignment. Paul had left Timothy in Ephesus with the important mission of preserving the doctrinal purity of the church there. The contents of this epistle show that Timothy was the leader of the whole church, responsible not only to maintain its doctrinal purity but also to appoint and supervise the elders and deacons.

Ephesus was religiously and politically the principle city of Asia Minor. Paul had labored there for more than two years. During this time, there was one of the most amazing movements of church growth in history, when the gospel radiated to all Asia (Acts 19:10), and churches were established all over the province. This was typical of Paul's strategy, to establish churches in key cities from which a witness could be initiated in surrounding areas.

Considering the importance of the church in Ephesus, its leader needed to be a key person. Timothy was given this assignment. Timothy was "urged" by Paul to stay on in Ephesus. The language suggests that Timothy had been reluctant to do so. His timid nature may have shrunk from such a big responsibility. Besides, he was still rather young (4:12). But Paul knew Timothy's abilities and, despite what seemed like numerous disqualifications, he gave him the job. This letter was among the things Paul did to encourage Timothy and buttress his authority. Paul probably expected this letter to be read out publicly in the churches in Asia. As the people heard this letter, they would know that Timothy was assigned the important role of leadership in the church by Paul himself.

Part of Timothy's duty was to "command certain men not to

teach false doctrines." The word translated "command" is a military term meaning "give strict orders." Because Timothy's position is an authoritative one, he could afford to act with authority. We can see how statements like this would help buttress Timothy's authority.

Here, incidentally, we also see the first of many suggestions given in this epistle about the attitude Timothy was to have toward false teaching (see 1 Tim. 1:3-11, 19, 20; 4:1-16; 6:3-5, 20, 21). Here, as elsewhere, Paul urged Timothy to take a firm stand. There can be no accommodating attitude on something so serious. False teachers were not to be allowed to teach in the church.

Preparing Timothy for Ministry. Paul could confidently hand over such a large work to Timothy because he had adequately invested his life in Timothy. Such preparation did not take place overnight or through a simple "leadership training course."

A native of Lystra, Timothy was probably converted during Paul's first missionary journey. When Paul came there on his second visit, he found Timothy highly esteemed by the Christian community. So Paul took him on to assist him in his travels (Acts 16:1-4).

During these years of Timothy's intimate contact with Paul, Timothy was able to observe Paul's life at close quarters. That life became an example for Timothy to follow. Paul said, "You, however, know all about my teaching, my way of life, my purpose, faith, patience, love, endurance, persecutions, sufferings" (2 Tim. 3:10, 11). The word translated here as *know* carries the idea of "tracing out as an example," of carefully noting "with a view to reproducing." It is a technical term, defining the relation of a disciple to his master.

Timothy knew exactly how Paul believed and taught, acted, and reacted, knowledge that was possible only because they had lived together, prayed together, studied the Word together, ministered together, and suffered together. During these experiences together, Paul had opened up his life to Timothy. Paul had adopted an openhearted approach to ministry. Of this approach Paul said, "We have spoken freely to you, Corinthians, and opened wide our hearts to you. We are not withholding our affection from you" (2 Cor. 6:11, 12; see also 1 Cor. 4:9).

This openhearted approach to ministry is not very common

today. Professionalism has so invaded today's approaches to ministry that pastors and teachers are encouraged to keep their personal, private lives and their ministry lives separate. They are taught not to expose their personal lives to those to whom they minister. Only in formal, prearranged meetings such as small groups, do they open up and share about their personal lives. Contact with people is limited to meetings and occasional personal appointments. By guarding their private lives, they will save themselves a lot of pain and trouble, they are told. But pain of exposure is the price of a deep ministry. Paul was willing to risk hurting himself by exposing himself to people like Timothy. And we know for a fact that because of such a close link with his spiritual children, he was hurt very often. But in the process he was able to multiply his ministry.

In my youth, I had the privilege of coming under the influence of two great disciplers, Sam Sherrard, our leader in Youth For Christ, and Robert Coleman, a seminary professor. Their personalities and methods of discipling were very different. But in many areas the way they ministered to me was the same. I had regular times of prayer and Bible study with them, usually along with a few others. They both had me over to their homes, again often along with a few others, to spend time with them and their families. We would often eat together and sometimes join in the work around the house. We would laugh together, discuss current affairs, sometimes argue about issues facing us, and very often, talk about the things of the Lord.

Both these men took me with them when they went out on ministry assignments. I observed them witnessing, counseling, conducting meetings, preaching, and responding to crises. Sometimes I was also given a small part in the program. Some of the best times we had were when we traveled to or from a place of ministry by train, bus, motorcycle, or car. During those conversations, they shared truths that went deep into my soul. Only in heaven will I know how much I learned from being with these two men of God.

So, during the times Timothy spent with Paul, he was able to observe Paul's life as an example to follow. During these times, Paul taught Timothy the basic truths of the Christian faith, as indicated in that famous text on the discipling ministry: "The things you have heard me say in the presence of many witnesses entrust to reliable men who will also be qualified to teach others" (2 Tim. 2:2). Here is described a body of truth that is to be passed down along four generations of Christians. During their times together, Paul had given Timothy a complete theological education. He had conducted a traveling Bible college.

This seems to be the way a lot of the ministers were trained during those days—not in the formal setting of a theological seminary, but in the setting of a ministry team, the way Jesus trained his disciples. I believe this is still the most effective way to train Christian workers. It is true that formal theological education is God's calling for some people, so I am not downplaying its value. But I believe we are often dumping on seminaries things that we should be doing, such as discipling leaders to maturity.

I believe the most effective environment for producing workers is a ministering team where vital body life is being experienced and where active ministry, careful supervision, and regular teaching is being done. Here soldiers are trained for battle on the battlefield itself. Such soldiers are best able to handle the warfare.

Some of the most effective evangelists I have met have had no formal theological training. Strangely, all of them seem to wish that they had taken some such training. But their ministry did not betray the need for it. They were people of the Word, with a passion for Christ, a burden for the lost, and a gift for preaching. They had learned to study the Word carefully and apply it relevantly to life. But notice that all of them spoke of an older evangelist who had taught them the Bible, and how to handle it, and how to proclaim it. They had been trained in the biblical way by men who believed in the ministry of multiplication. One thing they lacked was a certain type of recognition in certain circles. But the recognition we seek most is in heaven. And there we are recognized not for the quantity of our academic degrees but for the quality of our ministry.

Another key feature of Paul's training of Timothy had to do with the gradual handing over of some of his ministry to Timothy. The first record we have of this is during the first journey Timothy undertook with Paul. In Berea, Jews from Thessalonica stirred up the people so much that Paul had to leave the city. He left Timothy behind with the more senior man, Silas, to complete what needed to be done there (Acts 17:14, 15). Later on, Timothy was sent out on numerous missions as Paul's representative. Many of Paul's letters have Timothy's name along with his in the opening identification (2 Cor. 1:1; Phil. 1:1; Col. 1:1; 1 Thess. 1:1; 2 Thess. 1:1; Philem. 1:1). This fact shows that Paul was seeking to have the churches recognize Timothy as a key leader. It was a case of the senior man acting as the public relations officer of the junior man!

By the time 1 Timothy was written, Timothy was in charge of the large church in Ephesus. This church was such a big responsibility for a person his age that Timothy seemed reluctant to stick to it, so Paul had to urge him to continue in it (1 Tim. 1:3).

Paul could never have done such an amazing amount of work for the kingdom if he had not multiplied his ministry in people like Timothy. There is, of course, a price to pay in handing over ministries to younger assistants. They would not, at first, do the same high quality work as the leader. In fact, they may make some big mistakes that could jeopardize the reputation of the leader. Some may, on the other hand, end up overtaking the leader as far as prominence is concerned. This happened to the veteran Barnabas, who was later outshone by his young assistant, Paul. But the gospel moved out. A lasting work was accomplished. Churches were established. Capable men were left behind to lead them. And is not this what any minister would like to see accomplished from his ministry?

GIVING TIME FOR DISCIPLING

Concentrating upon just a few people in a discipling ministry is not very glamorous work. Discipling takes time, and many leaders are not willing to pay the price of giving so much of themselves in a private ministry such as discipling. Many leaders have too many public commitments to find time for discipling individuals.

Sometimes leaders complain that they are not able to develop leaders from their ministry because no one is willing to be trained. Yet the problem may be with the leader himself. He may have given people the impression that he is so busy that he cannot give time for extended individual discipling. As Leroy Eims puts it, "To have people become involved with you, you must first become involved with them" *(Lost Art)*. Eims calls this "a catch, a hidden factor" in the ministry of making disciples.

Leaders will have a constant battle in striking a balance between public ministry and personal discipling. Often the lure of public ministry can keep a leader from giving time for discipling. Walter Henrichsen has described this forcefully in his excellent book on the ministry of making disciples:

The discipling ministry lacks the glamour and excitement of the platform or large meeting type of ministry. But we can hardly overemphasize the importance of investing in the right kind of person, one of vision and discipline, totally committed to Jesus Christ, willing to pay any price to have the will of God fulfilled in his life. Sticking with a person and helping him to overcome the obstacles involved in becoming a disciple is a long and arduous task. (Disciples Are Made—Not Born, *Victor Books, 1974.)*

Discipling is a ministry many talk about today, but few practice in reality. Yet its importance cannot be exaggerated. This generation's best known mass evangelist underscores the importance of the ministry of discipling. In an interview published in the periodical, *Christianity Today,* Dr. Billy Graham was asked the question, "If you were a pastor of a large church in a principle city, what would be your plan of action?" Dr. Graham replied:

I think one of the first things I would do would be to get a small group of eight or ten or twelve men around me that would meet a few hours a week and pay the price! It would cost them something in time and effort. I would share with them everything I have, over a period of years. Then I would actually have twelve ministers among the laymen who in turn could take eight or ten or twelve more and teach them. I know one or two churches that are doing that, and it is revolutionizing the church. Christ, I think, set the pattern. He spent most of His time with twelve men. He didn't spend it with a great crowd. In fact, every time He had a great crowd it seems to me that there weren't too many results. The great results, it seems to me, came in His personal interview and in the time He spent with His twelve. (Quoted in Coleman, The Master Plan of Evangelism, *Revell, 1964.)*

PERSONAL APPLICATION

We should ask ourselves how much time we give per week for discipling younger Christians. Do we need to reorder our priorities so as to give more time for this ministry? Are there any decisions we need to make now about finding someone to disciple? We should pray about our personal response to this question.

TWO
THE VISION OF GRACE (1:11–17)

Our first chapter was about spiritual parenthood. In it we described human effort expended for the kingdom of God. A friend of mine, after reading a book with a similar message to that of the first chapter, complained that the book placed too much emphasis on human effort in the nurturing of believers and too little on God's grace. Paul presented to Timothy the concept of grace as the basis for all effective ministry. And in our study of this passage, we will discuss the different ways in which grace plays an important part in the Christian's life and ministry.

In 1:3-11 Paul responded to the false teaching which Timothy had to face in Ephesus. (We will not study this passage now, but later we will study a similar passage, 4:1-5.) At the conclusion of Paul's response, he referred to things that are "contrary to the sound doctrine that conforms to the glorious gospel of the blessed God, which he [God] entrusted to me" (1:10b, 11). There is a passing reference to Paul's call and ministry here. When Paul thought about his call and ministry, he also thought about the grace that lay behind that call and ministry (1:12-17).

GRACE IN CONVERSION AND MINISTRY (1:12-15)

In discussing his conversion and ministry, Paul used the word *grace* only once in these verses (12-15). Yet the idea of grace, as God's unmerited favor, is the main thrust of every statement here.

Called and Equipped (1:12). Paul gave three reasons why he was grateful to God about his ministry. He said, "I thank Christ Jesus our Lord, who has given me strength, that he considered me faithful, appointing me to his service" (1:12). Paul used three Greek verbs to describe his call and ministry, all in the aorist tense. The use of the aorist tense shows that Paul was referring to a definite moment in his spiritual pilgrimage when he received a call to ministry. The context shows that this took place in Paul's life at the time of his conversion.

Paul first said that the Lord Jesus "has given [him] strength." The verb Paul used *(endunamoo)* literally means to put strength within. When God called Paul to service, he invested him with sufficient strength to fulfill that call. God's servants are often hit with a sense of their own weakness as they are confronted by the demands of their ministry. But they are able to affirm that, though their strength may fail, God's strength will not. They may be struggling under the weight of responsibility, grappling to cope with the volume of work they have to do, or uncertain about their abilities. But they can always affirm, "The one who calls [us] is faithful and he will do it" (1 Thess. 5:24).

Secondly, Paul said that Christ "considered [him] faithful." The word used is sometimes translated "trustworthy." Paul could be relied on to faithfully carry out his responsibilities to the best of his abilities. Hiebert's comment on this clause is, "Not skill or knowledge but faithfulness is the first qualification for a minister of Christ" *(First Timothy, Everyman's Bible Commentary,* Moody, 1957). Paul said elsewhere, "It is required that those who have been given a trust must prove faithful" (1 Cor. 4:2).

Paul did not have some of the natural qualities we associate with a great preacher. He was gifted with a great mind, but he often said that he had less oratorical skills than others of his day (1 Cor. 2:1-5; 2 Cor. 10:10; 11:6). His physical appearance was weak (2 Cor. 10:10). He was often sick (2 Cor. 12:7-10; Gal. 4:13, 14). Yet he was faithful and willing to persevere, in spite of great difficulties, opposition, and strain (see 2 Cor. 4:7-12; 6:4-10; 11:23-29). This willingness was one of the keys to his ability to do so much lasting work for God.

William Carey, after being praised for his great achievements, was reported to have responded, "I'm just a plodder." Plodding— the willingness to stick to the work God has given until it is completed—lies at the heart of faithfulness in ministry. God saw this quality in Paul.

Yet a Christian's faithfulness, by itself, would be ineffective. Combined with God's strength, however, it becomes a powerful force in the service of the kingdom.

The third affirmation in this verse is that God followed through with his trust in Paul by "appointing [him] to his service." Paul was referring to a commission, a call to service, which he received at the time of his conversion. Though it was probably not a formal act as ordination, it was a word from God that he wanted him for service.

Few truths meant as much to me in my early Christian life (and even now) as the knowledge that God had called me to his service. I knew in theory that I was a child of God. But my nature found the implications of this sonship hard to accept. I struggled often with the feeling that I was inferior and worthless. Yet I had to reckon with the fact that I had been called, that God had considered me fit to do some work for him. This fact forced me into accepting and then enjoying the thrill of being God's child. I had believed in theory that I was precious to God, but his calling me into his service helped me sense it in practice. The thought is mind-boggling! The Lord of creation has something special for me to do for him!

The three statements of Paul, that Jesus had given him strength, that he had considered him faithful, and that he had appointed him to service, show us that Paul viewed his ministry primarily as a result of God's calling and equipping of him. This must surely have been a great source of encouragement and a motive to persevere through the many hardships and persecutions Paul faced. If the almighty God took the initiative to call Paul to himself and to his service, then surely he would continue to bless him, equip him and accomplish his purposes through him. No force, or circumstance, or opposition could override the effects of God's empowering for service.

Mercy to a Persecutor (1:13). Paul had just spoken about his call. In characteristic fashion, he immediately added something about his own unworthiness. He said he was called "even though [he] was a blasphemer and a persecutor and a violent man."

Some Christians glory in their pre-Christian sinful exploits.

When they share their testimony, they try to impress people with how bad they were. "I was a master at sin; I also had my fun," they seem to say. Their conversion pales into insignificance in the light of their colorful life of sin. People who hear them are left with an impression of sin, not of grace.

Paul also often used strong language to describe his preconversion behavior (see also 1 Cor. 15:9, Gal. 1:13, 14). But he always did it from the perspective of grace. His aim was to lift up grace, to show what a wonderful Savior Christ is. Referring to his preconversion behavior helped in fulfilling this aim, but it soon passed into the shadows as grace and mercy shone through.

Paul said, "I was shown mercy." The verb is in the passive voice, so we can translate it literally as, "I was mercied." By using the passive voice here, Paul is again lifting up grace. All the credit for his salvation went to God. Paul was an unworthy blasphemer, a persecutor, and a violent man. But in his wretched, helpless state, he was "mercied."

The word "mercy" (also used in verse 16) implies the former miserable state of the one being helped. It has a meaning similar to pity and compassion. "Grace" used in verse 14 implies that we don't deserve the help we receive. It is unmerited. Both words point to God's free provision to unworthy sinners.

Again, we affirm that Paul did not think about his conversion as a great decision he had made, but as a response to grace. Paul never said that he had chosen Christ, but always that Christ had chosen him.

A young person once said, "The Christian life does not work for me. I tried it, but I could not live up to my decision to follow Christ. In this condition, I did not want to be a hypocrite by calling myself a Christian, so I gave it up altogether." His focus had been on a decision he made to be a follower of Christ. For him, remaining a Christian had depended on his own heroic work. When he failed to live up to his decision, he felt he had to give up Christianity.

But the Christian life is entirely a response to grace. And the emphasis is on grace; not on our response or decision. This is why faith as small as a mustard seed is sufficient to live a powerful life (Luke 17:6). All that is needed is a response to God's grace. However feeble that response may be, God will take it and apply his powerful grace to it. It is right to view the Christian life as a partnership between grace and faith. But grace is the senior partner; the initiator and sustainer of the partnership.

So a vision of grace and mercy is a sign of healthy Christianity. It is very important, therefore, to impart this vision of grace to our spiritual children. Christian leaders may often have to tell younger believers things like, "Don't give up," "Make sure you have your devotional time," and "Don't give in to temptation." But these statements must be balanced by statements like, "God will help you," or "God's grace is greater than this temptation," or "You have been sealed for eternity by God's Holy Spirit."

Paul gave a reason why he was shown mercy. It was "because [he] acted in ignorance and unbelief" (1:13). This was no attempt to absolve himself of guilt. In the surrounding verses, Paul presented himself as the chief of sinners. Even in this verse Paul admitted to the basic sin of unbelief from which, Paul said elsewhere, arose all the other sins (Rom. 1:18-32). In this state of unbelief, said Paul, he was acting in ignorance. But when the truth was presented to him through the appearance of Christ at Damascus, and his eyes were opened to comprehend it, he immediately responded to it. It cost him dearly in terms of earthly security, status, and success. But he was willing to pay that price in the interests of truth.

There is a difference between sinners—even the chief of sinners, as Paul—who act in ignorance and those who deliberately reject the gospel after they have come to realize its truthfulness. For this the Pharisees were rebuked when they attributed to Beelzebub what was the clearly evident work of God through Christ (Matt. 12:22-37; Mark 3:20-30). Christ said that they were guilty of the unpardonable sin of blasphemy against the Holy Spirit. God cannot penetrate such people because they have closed their minds to the truth. For such there can be no hope of salvation. This is not because their sin is great, for God's grace is greater than all their sin. It is because they will not permit grace to act on them.

Super-abounding Grace (1:14a). Paul said, "The grace of our Lord was poured out on me abundantly, along with the faith and love that are in Christ Jesus" (1:14). "Poured out on me abundantly" is the translation of a single Greek word *(huperpleonasen),* which literally means "super-abounded."

Earlier, Paul had described his abounding sin. Here he presented God's super-abounding grace. Paul was constantly stirred by the "super" character of grace and redemption. He said in Romans 5:20, "where sin increased, grace increased all the more" (see also 2 Cor. 7:4; 12:7-10; Phil. 4:7; 2 Thess. 1:3). The chart below shows how the two themes of abounding sin and super-abounding grace criss-cross throughout the passage we are studying.

Abounding Sin	Super-abounding Grace
Blasphemer, persecutor, violent man (1:13a)	Mercy (1:13b), abounding grace (1:14)
Worst of sinners (1:15b)	Christ Jesus came to save sinners (1:15a)
Worst of sinners (1:16)	Mercy shown, the patience of God, an example for all (1:16)

This dual awareness of sin and grace is important to a healthy Christian experience. If the awareness of super-abounding grace is missing, we could be crushed when we realize the magnitude of our sin. An awareness of the greatness of his sin without a corresponding awareness of God's grace was probably what drove Judas to suicide.

When the powerful forces of evil assault us, we would wilt if we could not affirm amidst the confusion that grace is greater. Such confidence in grace helps us persevere along the path of obedience without bowing to the pressure of evil. We know God in Christ has dealt evil a decisive blow. Though for a time evil seems to have control of the situation, Christ will in the end emerge victor, and those who share in his grace will participate in that victory.

On the other hand, one who does not have a proper awareness of sin could never understand the glory of salvation. Many people who have grown up in a Christian background have such a problem. They think that by taking part in the Christian rituals or the so-called "means of grace," such as baptism and communion, they have merited God's favor. Little do they realize that the means of grace mediate grace only to those who have despaired of their ability to save themselves, repented of their sin, and trusted Christ alone for salvation.

The Evidence of Grace (1:14b). Paul said that grace was poured out on him, "along with faith and love in Christ Jesus" (1:14). Faith and love are coupled together many times in the New Testament epistles (Rom. 5:1-5; 1 Cor. 13:13; Gal. 5:5, 6; Eph. 1:15; 4:2-6; Col. 1:4, 5; 1 Thess. 1:3; 5:8; 2 Thess. 1:3; Philem. 4; Heb. 6:10-12, 10:22-24; 1 Pet. 1:3-8, 21, 22). Faith is reliance upon God in every situation of life. It is entrusting ourselves to God, believing what the Scriptures say about him, and knowing that he can and will save and provide for us.

Love is the direct result of faith. When we place our faith in God, we enter into his family. Or as Paul said in this verse, we are "in Christ Jesus." That is, we enter into the sphere of his activity. Then God's love is poured out into our hearts (Rom. 5:5). As we in faith surrender our whole life to God, his love is able to transform our nature and work itself out in our behavior. We become loving people. Paul described this process as "faith expressing itself through love" (Gal. 5:6). So Christian love is not primarily what we do in response to God's grace. It is more a result of entering the sphere of God's activity ("in Christ Jesus") and letting his qualities become part of us by opening or surrendering our lives to him.

The fact that the New Testament epistles use faith and love so often to describe genuine Christianity shows us that they are the two most important evidences of Christian conversion. Not all who profess to place their trust in Christ have exercised saving faith. The genuineness of the conversion is shown when faith and love are put to the test.

Does a person revert to his old religion or superstitions at a time of persecution or crisis? Then his faith is not genuine. Does a person seek revenge when he is wronged? Or think only of his own welfare? Then his love is not genuine. Only God really knows who is saved and who is not. But faith and love are generally reliable evidences of the reality of conversion.

The Heart of the Gospel (1:15). Paul came to the very heart of the gospel: "Here is a trustworthy saying that deserves full acceptance: Christ Jesus came into the world to save sinners—of whom I am the worst." Up to then, he had been talking of grace and mercy. Here he came to the event that made this grace and mercy available.

It was the coming of Christ that made man's salvation possible. Paul explained this further by saying that Christ Jesus "gave himself as a ransom for all men" (2:6). A price had to be paid for our freedom. By dying on the cross, Jesus paid this price. Through that act, grace was made available to us.

The sequence of this passage is significant. Paul made a passing reference to his calling, and further a reference to the grace that lay behind that call. His meditation on it led him in turn to the event that lay behind the grace, which was the coming of Christ. Thinking on this grace caused an attitude of adoration to well up in Paul's mind, which moved him to an outpouring of praise to God (v. 17).

Paul related the gospel to himself by saying he was "the worst" of the sinners Christ came to save. Paul often used superlatives to describe his unworthiness (1 Cor. 15:9; Eph. 3:8). The more Paul understood of the magnitude of grace the more conscious he became of his sinfulness. With Paul this was not a case of mock modesty, for on other occasions he did not hesitate to commend his own obedience to God, as in Acts 23:1; 24:16; 2 Corinthians 11:5; 12:11; and Galatians 2:6.

GRACE IN EVANGELISTIC PREACHING

From the above verses, we can imply that grace needs to be an important topic in our evangelistic preaching. We must declare to people that Christ has done everything necessary for their salvation and that all they need to do is to open their lives to the blessings of God by turning from their past lives and letting Christ be their Savior and Lord.

Yet the idea of grace, though simple to grasp, goes against the grain of normal human thinking. Buddhists, for example, find the idea of grace very difficult to accept. Merit is a key concept in Buddhism. Merit is earned by human effort. As the Dhammapada puts it, "Purity and impurity depend on oneself. No one can purify another" (verse 165). Christianity, on the other hand, affirms that "the blood of Jesus . . . purifies us from every sin" (1 John 1:7). All the merit for our salvation belongs to Christ. The Buddhist sees this as a cheap salvation and an encouragement to continue in sin.

The Hindus are more open to the concept of grace. In certain forms of Hinduism there is even a belief that salvation or liberation occurs through the grace of God *(prasada)*, where God is seen as short-circuiting the effect of *karma*. This belief is common in the Bhakti movement of Hinduism, a movement that places emphasis on loving adoration and devotion to God.

Yet, even among the Bhakti theologians, there is division about the importance of grace. As Ninian Smart observes, "One doctrine was that liberation is entirely the work of the Lord; the other that moral (and also in some cases ritual) effort is necessary to qualify for grace" ("Hindu Concept of Grace," *Dictionary of Comparative Religion,* Charles Scribner's Sons, 1970).

Mahatma Gandhi is a good example of Hindu reluctance to accept the Christian doctrine of grace. Gandhi was deeply influenced both by the Hindu Bhakti movement and by the life of Christ, whom he regarded as "a beautiful example of the perfect man." Gandhi was deeply impressed by the Sermon on the Mount and sought to follow its teachings. He viewed Christ as "a martyr, an embodiment of sacrifice" and his death as "a great example to the world." But he would not go beyond that. He was not ready "to believe literally that Jesus by his death and by his blood redeemed the sins of the world." He was concerned that the Christian concept of grace would be a source of moral license. (For a summary of Gandhi's views on Christ, see M. M. Thomas' book, *The Acknowledged Christ of the Indian Renaissance,* London: SCM Press, 1969.)

Gandhi's attitude is typical of the heights that man can reach in his fallen state. The essence of fallenness is the attempt to be independent from God. Man wants to decide for himself what to him will be good and what will be evil. This is what the forbidden fruit signified (Gen. 3:5, 22). So, even the best of fallen men want to save themselves by their own efforts, independent of God's help.

Gandhi sought salvation in the pursuit of truth *(satya)* through non-violence *(ahimsa)*. The Buddhist seeks salvation or *nirvana* through "the noble eightfold path." The person from a Christian background may strive for it through penance, rituals, baptism, churchmanship, or even good citizenship. He wants to do something for his salvation. So grace is a concept that fallen man independent from God finds difficult to accept.

Into such an environment we are called to proclaim the gospel of grace. And not only to proclaim it, but also to persuade or convince people of its truth (see Acts 17:2-4; 18:4, 13; 24:25; 26:28; 28:23, 24; 2 Cor. 5:11). This challenge is one of the most absorbing that today's evangelist faces. He must respond to objections brought against the concept. He must be able to demonstrate that in grace alone lies man's hope. He must by analogy explain what his alien concept of grace means, using illustrations drawn from daily life. He must announce what Christ has done on behalf of man.

Billy Graham was right when he insisted that an evangelistic sermon is incomplete without reference to the Cross of Christ. We would add that such a sermon is ineffective if it does not convince the hearer that what Christ did on the cross is his only hope for salvation. This is true not only in the cases of sermons, but also in our personal witnessing to unbelievers.

WE ARE EXAMPLES OF GRACE (1:16)

After declaring the heart of the gospel which saved him, Paul explained why he, of all people, was given such a prominent place in its history. He said, "But for that very reason I was shown mercy so that in me, the worst of sinners, Christ Jesus might display his unlimited patience as an example for those who believe on him and receive eternal life" (1:16).

Paul said he was an "example" of God's great grace. This word translated "example" *(hupotuposin)* literally means "outline sketch." Before doing a painting an artist normally prepares a sketch to set down his main ideas. In the same way, early in the history of the church, Christ used Paul to "display" to the world an "example" of what he was going to do in millions of lives. The word "display," which could also be translated as "exhibit," is also a striking word.

Paul's point was that if a sinner as bad as he could be saved, then there is hope for anyone. Salvation depends on God's mercy. All we have to do to appropriate it is to "believe on him."

Paul said that mercy manifests itself in "unlimited patience." Man deserves to be destroyed at once. But God patiently waits for him to repent (see Rom. 2:4). By using the expression "unlimited patience," Paul did not imply that everybody will be ultimately saved, for this same verse says that salvation is for those who believe in Christ. God's patience is unlimited in that no sin is too big to forgive.

But on man's side, there must be repentance. If man refuses to repent then he will not receive salvation. So, in his letter to the Romans, just after speaking of God's patience, Paul said, "But because of your stubbornness and your unrepentant heart, you are storing up wrath against yourself for the day of God's wrath" (Rom. 2:5). For this reason, "unlimited" may not be the best translation for the word Paul used in 1:16, which literally means "all." Yet for those who believe, there is always hope. However sinful they may have been, they will have eternal life.

Anyone involved in evangelism will soon find people who think there is no hope for them, that they are too far gone in the life of sin. This passage says there is hope for everyone. R. A. Torrey gave the example of such a person in his classic book, *Personal Work* (Revell). After a Sunday morning service, Dr. Torrey asked an able and intelligent man, "Are you a real Christian?"

"I am too great a sinner to be saved," he replied.

Dr. Torrey read to him 1 Timothy 1:15, about how Christ Jesus came into the world to save sinners and how Paul said that he was the chief of sinners.

The man said, "Well, I am the chief of sinners."

"That verse means you, then," said Torrey. The man realized there was hope for him. When Dr. Torrey asked him whether he would accept Christ's salvation, he immediately knelt down, confessed his sin, and asked God's forgiveness. Soon he confessed Christ publicly. His broken home was restored, and he became a witnessing Christian.

Now there is a sense in which all Christian leaders are examples of grace to others. Our example may not be as spectacular as Paul's. Yet it is significant, for all of us were undeserving sinners before our conversion. Just as Paul lifted up grace often by referring to his testimony, so must we. When our spiritual children observe us, the biggest impression they get should be of the greatness of God's grace.

FROM GRACE TO PRAISE (1:17)

At the end of Paul's reflection on the grace of God, he broke forth into spontaneous praise to God: "Now to the King eternal, immortal, invisible, the only God, be honor and glory for ever and ever. Amen." This doxology (statement of praise) is one of the many to be found in Paul's letters (see 6:16; 2 Tim. 4:18; Rom. 11:33-36; 16:27; Gal. 1:5; Eph. 3:21; Phil. 4:20).

Praise is a natural result of focusing on the grace of God. Grace reminds us of all Christ has done. But as we become engrossed in the responsibilities of this life, it is easy to forget what Christ has done. When this happens, our praise seems unnatural and forced.

Being too much caught up in the things of this life may be the reason why praise does not come naturally to so many of us Christians. We have lost the vision of grace by letting the cares of life crowd it out of our thinking. To bring grace back into the picture we need to give time to meditating on it, to recalling God's goodness to us, to counting our blessings. As we do, we will find it easier to go about life with an attitude of praise.

PERSONAL APPLICATION

Using insights gained from this passage and elsewhere, list ways in which you can communicate the vision of grace to your spiritual children.

THREE
INSTRUCTION AND DISCIPLING (1:18–20)

The main reason for Paul's first and second letters to Timothy was to instruct Timothy about his various duties. Some seventy-five specific instructions can be found in these two epistles. The fact that Paul gives such specific commands to his disciple Timothy shows us that a Christian leader is responsible to instruct those he leads. First Timothy 1:18-20 provides a base to study how one should exercise this ministry of instruction.

HOW TO INSTRUCT (1:18a)

Paul began: "Timothy, my son, I give you this instruction" (1:18). The word "instruction" *(parangelia),* sometimes translated "charge," is a strong word used in military contexts to convey a sense of urgent obligation. This noun and its corresponding verb occur seven times in 1 Timothy (1:3, 5, 18; 4:11; 5:7; 6:13, 17). Paul also used another word, "urge" or "exhort" *(parakaleo),* to refer to instruction in 1 and 2 Timothy (1 Tim. 1:3; 2:1; 5:1; 6:2; 2 Tim. 4:2). These words carry the idea of specific instructions given for specific situations.

In the second epistle, Paul gave Timothy some guidelines on how he should instruct: "Preach the Word; be prepared in season and out of season; correct, rebuke and encourage—with great patience and careful instruction" (2 Tim. 4:2). Our first and most important responsibility is to "preach the Word." The discipler is not to guide a person with his own ideas. Rather, he is to help him to apply the Word of God to his life. Whatever instruction he gives must accord with the Word. The Word itself is the most important part of the instruction.

Preaching the Word, however, does not fully cover the complete ministry of instruction. Often the spiritual parent finds that in spite of his faithful proclamation of the Word, his spiritual child falls into sin and error. Then he must "correct, rebuke, and exhort." The word "correct" used here, translated sometimes "use argument," points to an intellectual approach to error. Others, whose errors are more moral than intellectual, need to be rebuked. They have sinned and must be censured. Still others need to be exhorted. This word carries the idea of urging people on. These three words give a good summary of the way practical instructions should be given. As E. F. Scott said in his comment on this verse, "The discipler's ministry involves an appeal to the reason, the conscience, and the will" *(The Pastoral Epistles,* London: Hodder and Stoughton, 1936). Next Paul gave two more qualities that need to go hand in hand with instruction: "with great patience and careful instruction" (2 Tim. 4:2). A good instructor needs to be patient. Without patience one could crush a sensitive soul when rebuking him.

A disciple maker must teach. The Greek word translated "instruction" is *didache,* the most commonly used word for teaching. It is not enough to simply tell a person, "Do this. Don't do that. . . ." That type of instruction will produce a robot—someone who does things only by rote. God has given us minds which he intends us to use in the Christian life. The vibrant disciple needs to know the reason why he does or doesn't do certain things. Therefore, if he is rebuked for wrongdoing, he must be told why he was wrong.

A thinking Christian will find it difficult to take correction, rebuke, and exhortation for very long unless there is teaching to go along with it. New believers may tolerate it for a time because of their eagerness to grow in their newfound faith. But after a while, they will react against it, which explains why some young people turn against their disciplers. They want something more than robotlike direction. They want reasons. And there are reasons, for Christianity is a reasonable faith.

Yet a far more common error in discipling is the opposite error to the one we have just described. Disciplers who may be faithful in teaching often neglect their duty to give specific instructions and point out wrong in the lives of their spiritual children. They see weaknesses and failings, misconceptions, and wrong ideas in the disciples' lives, but they avoid the unpleasant work of pointing these out. Some even say it is none of their business to be prying into other people's affairs in this way. Paul would certainly have considered such an attitude as selfish.

To see a person in error or in need of direction and to do nothing about it is considered in the Bible a very serious sin. God told Ezekiel, "When I say to a wicked man, 'You will surely die,' and you do not warn him or speak out to dissuade him from his evil ways in order to save his life, that wicked man will die for his sin, and I will hold you accountable for his blood" (Ezek. 3:18).

INSTRUCTING WITH AN AMBITIOUS SPIRIT (1:18b)

Paul spoke of the prophecies made about Timothy: "My son, I give you this instruction in keeping with the prophecies once made about you." Paul apparently knew of a special message from God, given at Timothy's ordination or perhaps before, which affirmed that Timothy had a bright future as an effective minister. Paul's confidence about Timothy's future formed the basis of his ambitions for Timothy. When Paul instructed Timothy he did it with these ambitions in view. He believed that his instructions were going to help Timothy achieve the great things God had in store for him.

Such a desire for the spiritual success of our spiritual children is another important aspect of the discipling ministry. We are to be ambitious for our spiritual children and our actions are to be aimed at helping them to achieve all God desires for them. In fact, Paul was not reluctant to remind Timothy of his great potential (see also 4:12-14; 2 Tim. 1:5-7). One can imagine how such words would have encouraged the self-effacing Timothy to strive for higher things.

None of us may ever receive a direct prophecy from God to form the basis of our ambitions for our spiritual children. But we may arrive at a "prophetic insight," a dream of what God can do through them. This may come to us through observation or through our discerning the particular gifts these individuals may have received from the Holy Spirit. Such words of "prophetic insight" by three Christian leaders did much to sustain and encourage me in my early years as a Christian.

Some disciplers don't reflect in their instructions such an ambition for the personal development of those they are discipling. Sometimes the disciple gets the idea that the one discipling him thinks he is so incapable that he must be told everything he is to do. Such instruction tends to devastate an insecure person by causing him to lose all confidence in his abilities. Others would resent being treated like little children and after a while end up avoiding the discipler.

Sometimes the young Christian gets the idea from the way he is being instructed that true personal concern is lacking. He is made to feel that his only importance lies in the fact that by allowing himself to be discipled he helps the organization or church to which he belongs to achieve one of its goals. The instruction primarily concerns the way he is doing his job in the committee or in whatever such group he is a member. Such instruction of course will not produce mature disciples.

So we see how important it is for disciplers to have ambitions for those they disciple, ambitions which influence the entire discipling process.

INSTRUCTING TO HELP
FIGHT THE GOOD FIGHT (1:18c)

Paul stated as his immediate aim: "I give you this instruction . . . so that by following them you may fight the good fight." The prophecies we talked of above will brace Timothy to help him fight the good fight. So Paul's aim was to provoke Timothy to maintain his warrior mentality.

The Christian life is a battle against the forces of evil and on behalf of the Kingdom of God. Yet, it is easy for a Christian to lose the warrior mentality and to settle down to an ordinary "civilian life." We are all naturally prone to lethargy. There almost seems to be a secret law of the soul that if we stop battling as warriors, lethargy sets in. It may hit us in our prayer life or in our Bible study, in our battle against bad thoughts, or in our discretion in relationships with members of the opposite sex, in our concern for our home, or in our studies, in our witnessing, or as we try to maintain Christian standards in our workplace.

The spurring on of another Christian may be all that is needed to reverse the trend towards lethargy in one's life. Just a simple question like, "How is your devotional life?" can jolt him enough to get him back to the discipline of prayer and Bible study. The writer of Hebrews showed that Christian friends should play a significant role in helping others to avoid lethargy: "Let us consider how we can spur one another on towards love and good deeds" (Heb. 10:24).

Spurring people on in the Christian warfare is one of the greatest values of discipling. A believer being accountable to another person is often a great deterrent to lethargy. Discipling fosters this sense of accountability. The aim of spurring Timothy on seemed to have been on Paul's mind constantly as he wrote these letters. They are full of rousing calls to alertness and total discipleship (1 Tim. 4:11-16; 6:11-16; 2 Tim. 1:6-14; 2:1-26; 4:1-5).

ARMOR FOR THE WARFARE (1:19a)

Paul then described the armor that is required for Christian warfare (1:19a). Timothy was to fight "holding on to faith and a good conscience." Faith—right beliefs—was an essential. If he believed the wrong things, he would not battle properly. Over and over again in these epistles, Paul underlined the need for correct beliefs. In the last chapter we saw how one's belief in the doctrine of grace is so vital for healthy Christianity.

Next, Paul said that Timothy must be armed with a good conscience, that is, he must be sensitive to God's voice. His conscience should be penetrable. If his conscience has been hardened by pride or a sense of self-sufficiency, or defensiveness, no one can get through to him. He would not accept his faults. He would not see areas in his life that needed to be improved. It would be difficult to advise him and more difficult to rebuke him. For people with such hardened consciences there is little hope of spiritual progress because God cannot penetrate their minds. This fact explains why Paul described those who had rejected faith and a good conscience as having "shipwrecked their faith" (1:19b). The only solution with such people may be to take the type of drastic step of excommunication which Paul said he took with Alexander and Hymenaeus (1:20).

What a contrast to these people Timothy was! Though he was a highly placed leader, he remained teachable enough for Paul to feel free to instruct him in such a comprehensive way in these two letters.

LEADERSHIP AND DISCIPLINE (1:19b, 20)

Paul named two people, Hymenaeus and Alexander, who shipwrecked their faith by rejecting faith and a good conscience (1:20). These men Paul said he had "handed over to Satan, to be taught not to blaspheme." This expression "handed over to Satan" (also found in 1 Cor. 5:5) is used to denote excommunication. It refers to "the expulsion of the sinner from the Church, the realm of God's care and protection, and the formal handing over of him to the power of Satan" (J. N. D. Kelly, *A Commentary on the Pastoral Epistles,* London: Adams & Charles Black, 1963).

This type of discipline was practiced regularly in the early church. Paul rebuked the Corinthians for their slowness to take action against a member who was guilty of incest: "And you are proud! Shouldn't you rather have been filled with grief and have put out of your fellowship the man who did this? . . . 'Expel the wicked man from among you' " (1 Cor. 5:2, 13). Here Paul recommended excommunication for immorality. Alexander and Hymenaeus were excommunicated for blasphemy (1 Tim. 1:2). Writing to Titus, Paul recommended disciplinary action when people caused disunity due to false teaching. Paul said, "Avoid foolish controversies and genealogies and arguments and quarrels about the law. . . . Warn a divisive person once, and then warn him a second time. After that have nothing to do with him" (Titus 3:9, 10). Paul recommended somewhat milder treatment for anyone in Thessalonica who did not obey the instructions in his epistle. "Do not associate with him, in order that he may feel ashamed. Yet do not regard him as an enemy, but warn him as a brother" (2 Thess. 3:14, 15).

We see from the above references that the intensity of the disciplinary punishment may vary. But in each case it is clear that wrong belief and practice are regarded with utmost seriousness in the church.

This serious attitude toward sin was essential if there was to be true repentance. In fact, one of the main reasons for the exercise of discipline in the early church was to open the door for repent-

ance. So, Hymenaeus and Alexander were handed over to Satan
so that they may be "taught not to blaspheme."

The sinner in Corinth was to be handed over to Satan "so that
the sinful nature may be destroyed and his spirit saved on the day
of the Lord" (1 Cor. 5:5). The disobedient one of Thessalonica
was to be left alone "in order that he may feel ashamed" (2 Thess.
3:14). Paul seemed to be implying that no true repentance and
healing after sin is possible until the gravity of the sin has been
faced squarely.

Often Christians fall into sin and try to cover it up or confess
only part of their wrongdoing—usually that part which is clearly
open to public view and thus cannot be denied. John Bunyan
referred to men who "confess sins notionally and by halves." He
said that this was "dangerous, because the wound is healed
falsely" *(Upon a Penny Loaf,* compiled by Roger Palms, Bethany
Fellowship, 1978). Many Christians today are carrying falsely
healed wounds. They have sinned but have not fully accepted the
responsibility for their sin. Therefore, they have not experienced
God's complete forgiveness. Yet they have been accepted into the
fellowship and pursue their activity in the Christian community.
But they could never live a life which fully pleases God. They have
built around themselves a barrier which prevents them from being
fully open to God or to others. The barrier hinders their spiritual
growth. They are prone to compromise in a crisis because their
sensitivity to sin has been blunted. A loss of a sensitive conscience
is one of the most serious harms to result from the neglect of
proper disciplinary action. A dull conscience closes the door to
healing after sin and it opens the door to compromise and half-
hearted commitment.

One of the hardest tasks of a leader is to direct those under his
care who have sinned to see the gravity of their sin and to face its
consequences. Such a task is often unpleasant, especially when
the person denies the sin or offers excuses to acquit himself.
Under such pressure leaders often back off and let the matter rest
there. But sin not properly dealt with doesn't just rest there. It
works its way into the life of the Christian, stunting his growth and
then affecting the whole community.

The discipler must seek to cultivate an atmosphere in which sin
is regarded as very serious and where believers learn to listen to
the voice of God speaking through their consciences, where they

know that rejecting their responsibility to holy living results in the loss of the blessings of fellowship. Such an atmosphere promotes the quality of spiritual life that brings glory to our holy God.

The rest of 1 Timothy contains instructions on various topics that relate to Timothy's life and ministry as listed below:

2:1-8	Praying during worship
2:9-15	Women in worship
3:1-13	Qualifications for overseers and deacons
3:14-16	Why these instructions are so important
4:1-11	How to respond to false teaching
4:12-16	How to respond when criticized (with an exemplary life and ministry)
5:1, 2	How to relate to old and young men and women
5:3-16	The care of widows
5:17-25	The choice and supervision of elders
5:23	Timothy's physical health
6:1, 2	How servants should relate to masters
6:3-5	What false teachers are like
6:6-10	Christian attitude to possessions and ambition
6:11-16	Timothy's personal battle for holiness
6:17-19	How to instruct the rich about possessions
6:20	A final charge

What a varied list this is! There is advice on physical health and spiritual life, on practical ministry and doctrinal belief. It is a reflection of how comprehensive the leader's concern should be for his spiritual children.

PERSONAL APPLICATION

Make a list of the instructions on different topics you need to give to those you lead. Write down when you hope to give these instructions. By writing these facts down, you are more likely to be motivated to do what you have written about.

FOUR
ASPIRING TO
LEADERSHIP (3:1, 2, 7)

Anyone who does a biblical study of leadership would do well to consider 1 Timothy chapter 3 because it presents clearly the qualifications for leadership in the church. It deals with three groups of leaders: "overseers" (3:1-7), "deacons" (3:8-10, 12, 13) and "women" who are leaders (3:11). The last group could either be deaconesses or the wives of deacons. In this book we will study only Paul's discussion of overseers, as studying that role gives a clear and comprehensive description of what a leader should be.

OVERSEERS AND DEACONS

Paul's discussion of overseers is often taken to apply only to an elite group of top-level church leaders because some of the older English translations refer to this group as "bishops." Most Christians today think of a bishop as a person who oversees a large number of churches covering a wide geographical area or diocese.

In the New Testament Epistles, the title "bishop," or overseer, was used for those who had pastoral oversight of local churches. The Greek word *episkopos* means "one who oversees." In fact, as in Philippi, some local churches had more than one overseer (Phil. 1:1). So there is some justification for the *Today's English Version*'s very general rendering of *episkopos* as "church leader."

Overseers were also called "elders" *(presbuteros;* Titus 1:6, 7;

Acts 20:17, 28) and "pastors" *(poimen;* Eph. 4:11). "Overseer" and "pastor" are titles related to the function of the leader. He is one who oversees and feeds God's flock. "Elder" is a title related to his being a senior person in the church.

The term "deacon" *(diakonos)* means one who serves. In the early days of the church, as recorded in Acts, they were responsible for the proper distribution of food to all the people of the church. In second-century Christian literature, there were two functions ascribed often to deacons: the administration of church funds and house-to-house visitation. This was probably the type of work deacons did in Timothy's time also.

ASPIRE TO LEADERSHIP (3:1a)

Before presenting his list of qualifications for leaders, Paul encouraged Christians to aspire to leadership: "Here is a trustworthy saying: If anyone sets his heart on being an overseer, he desires a noble task."

Two expressions here describe a Christian who aspires to leadership. The first, "sets his heart on," literally means "stretches himself after." The word implies that some effort is exerted. This word is translated elsewhere as "aspires," which better captures the meaning. An aspiring leader struggles to overcome his weaknesses and to acquire the Christlike character described in verses 2-7. He grows in his knowledge of the Word and of the world. And he develops skills of communicating God's truth effectively to his generation.

Paul's second word for aspiration, "desires," presents leadership as a goal one places before him with great longing. The New English Bible renders it as "ambition." Christian ambition, however, is not the same as selfish ambition. Christian ambition arises out of a desire to be used by God to the fullest. The primary goal toward which a Christian strives is to be totally available for God to use as he sees fit. Leadership is a very effective way of being used by God as it provides a wide sphere of influence for good, the prospect of which should motivate a Christian to aspire for leadership.

A Christian also knows that at the heart of leadership is servanthood. We are followers of a servant Lord (Luke 22:27), who was gentle and lowly in heart (Matt. 11:29). Jesus told his disciples,

"Whoever wants to become great among you must be your servant, and whoever wants to be first must be your slave" (Matt. 20:26, 27). A true Christian knows that the moment he becomes proud, he forfeits his right to lead. As he aspires to leadership, then, he will be alert to the possibility of pride, which lies at the heart of selfish ambition.

A Christian may aspire to leadership, yet since his primary desire is to be obedient to Christ, he will be completely satisfied even if God's will for him does not include leadership. His satisfaction springs from God and from doing his will. Such a person will be happy in whatever task God may lead him to do.

A NOBLE TASK (3:1b)

The Significance of the Ministry. When Paul described the work of an overseer as "a noble task," he was trying to increase the esteem attached to the ministry and thus to attract good men to offer themselves for the position.

The ministry brought with it numerous problems, and it involved hard work. It opened the person to the prospect of persecution and criticism. Christians in Ephesus in Timothy's time were an economically poor minority. So, however hard they worked, those serving the church in a full-time capacity would not have had much opportunity to climb in society, either economically or in status.

Later in this epistle, Paul insisted that overseers should be adequately paid (5:17). But Paul's measure of adequate provision was nowhere near what we would equate with prosperity. He said, "If we have food and clothing we will be content with that" (6:8). Paul himself had earthly status and riches before his conversion. But he gave all that up when he became a servant of Christ (see Phil. 3:4-9).

Yet Paul had no doubt of the fact that Christian ministry was "a noble task." "Noble" is a word for status. The minister's status does not come from possessions or position in society. It comes from the great significance of the work he is doing. He is dispensing the greatest treasure in the world, the eternal gospel, on which alone lies man's hope for salvation. He is an ambassador of the King of all the earth. And the appeal this King makes to the world, he makes through him (2 Cor. 5:20).

The Christian ministry is a noble work, to be done with joy, even with unselfish pride. The pay and earthly status it brings may not be substantial. Yet Paul had no hesitation to ask people to aspire to it, to give stiff qualifications for entrance into it, and to demand utmost care in the choice of ministers (see also 5:22). Such approaches to recruitment usually apply to very important jobs. And this truly is an important job!

In many countries today, where Christians are an economically poor minority, the church suffers much from unmotivated workers who do low-quality work. One reason for this fact is that they have lost the sense of the glory of their ministry. A person will enthusiastically devote his full energies and creativity to a work which he regards as highly significant. But many ministers, influenced by the false standards of society, have lost a sense of the importance of their ministry. As a result, there is a drop in their level of motivation and then in the quality of their work.

Seeing this sad state of affairs, many bright young Christians are turned off to the idea of considering the ministry as a vocation. A few months ago, such a young person told me, "I would like to join the full-time ministry. But most of the ministers in my denomination seem to be unenthusiastic and unmotivated. I just don't want that to happen to me. So I think I'll serve God as a layman."

How important it is for us to retrieve the glory that rightly belongs to the ministry! If we are gripped by the significance of what we are doing, the quality of our work will go up. Sloppy work is incompatible with the great gospel of which we are bearers, and with the God of the gospel whose ambassadors we are. As the quality of our ministry goes up, the esteem for the ministry in the church will also go up. Soon we may find outstanding young men and women responding to God's call to full-time ministry.

Feeling Sorry for Ministers. Because the ministry is so glorious a calling, ministers must not expect people to feel sorry for them. There is nothing to be sorry about. Yet Christian workers often seek the pity of those outside the ministry. They show this most often by talking about their difficulties. It is not wrong to share our problems with fellow Christians, but it is wrong to do it in such a way that causes people to lose sight of the glory of the ministry. It is wrong because we are not telling the truth.

Why do some ministers, in their conversations, overemphasize the problems of their ministry? Sometimes they do so to impress people with the sacrifices they have made, so we hear statements like, "If I had continued with my secular job, I would be earning $ _____ now."

Sometimes ministers talk about their problems to counter criticism against their ministry. "You say we don't work hard enough," a minister might say, "but look at what a difficult life we have to live."

A third reason ministers talk about their problems is to try to get assistance from laymen to help with their difficulties. Assisting each other is an important aspect of Christian community life. The one with two coats has a responsibility to give to the one who has none (Luke 3:11). But ministers should beware of trying to maneuver others into helping them, especially with financial assistance. Some affluent Christians help out ministers financially purely out of a sense of guilt over their relative prosperity. Some feel they have been pressured into giving by being made aware of the minister's need in a way that embarrasses them into responding.

The goodwill that comes from this type of giving will soon turn sour and the giver will lose his respect for the minister. The minister thus loses his authority and the freedom he needs to minister effectively. It will become difficult to exhort and rebuke people to whom he feels certain obligations because of what they have done for him.

A good example of how the glory of ministry overshadows the cost of ministry comes from the life of David Livingstone, a man who laid aside a medical career in Scotland to go to Africa as a missionary. For years he labored there, often alone, amidst many hardships. "He was attacked and maimed by a lion, his home was destroyed during the Boer war, his body was often racked by fever and dysentery, and his wife died on the field" (Elmer Towns, *The Christian Hall of Fame*, Baker, 1971). A lady once commented to Livingstone about how much he had sacrificed for the gospel. Livingstone, angered by this comment, is said to have responded, "Sacrifice? The only sacrifice is to live outside the will of God!"

All the sacrifices we make are overshadowed by the glory of doing the will of God. If a sense of this glory has not overshadowed our difficulties and problems, then the cost of ministry will appear to us to be very big. The next step would be to dwell on the sacrifices we have made.

A sense of the glory of ministry will show us that we are un-worthy servants entrusted with a noble work, as jars of clay holding a great treasure. We have not given up anything significant. We have actually been exalted to a position far beyond what we deserve. So, rather than being sorry for ourselves, we should be thanking God for blessings we do not deserve.

THE LEADER'S REPUTATION (3:2, 7)

After a passing reference to the glory of the overseer's task, Paul presented a list of fifteen qualifications necessary for those holding that position (3:2-7). He began with the word *dei,* which in the original means literally, "it is necessary." This word is rendered "must be" in most English translations. Paul was stating that the position and responsibilities of leadership are such that one who wishes to be a leader must possess these basic qualifications.

In our study, we are arranging Paul's list of qualifications for leadership topically. Paul gives two social qualifications that have to do with the prospective leader's reputation. He gives only one ministry qualification—the ability to teach. Eight qualifications deal with the person's behavior, three with his family life, and one with his spiritual maturity ("not . . . a recent convert").

1. Reputation with Christians (3:2). The first social qualification is that a leader "must be above reproach." Literally this could be translated, "not to be laid hold of." An adversary looking for a fault should find no faults within the Christian leader to use against him. The next few verses amplify this statement by stating in what areas the leader should be above reproach. As verse 7 refers to the leader's "good reputation with outsiders" or non-Christians, we can assume that Paul was referring here to his reputation with Christians.

There is a great need in the church today for leaders with untainted reputations. One of the biggest crises facing the church is the question of godliness. Believers struggle with the question of whether it is really possible to be totally committed to Christ in today's world. Because of evil's great power in our society, many Christians feel it is not possible to survive without compromising some Christian standards. As a result, they have settled for a substandard Christian life.

If Christian leaders also fail here, the weak find an excuse for their own failure. Although they may not say so openly, many of them ask themselves, "If the leaders can't follow the principles of the Bible, how do you expect us to be able to follow them?" They note the leaders' failures and store these facts to use as a weapon to justify their own lack of complete dedication.

Yet Christ said, "Be perfect . . . as your heavenly Father is perfect" (Matt. 5:48), which is the norm for the Christian. The command implies that we are expected to live with a conscience that is void of offense before men and before God. It implies that we should be totally obedient in everything we know to be the will of God. It implies that sin, however small, is never excusable for a Christian. In an age when most Christians don't think such commands can be followed completely, Christian leaders are called to demonstrate these truths to the church.

If leaders live exemplary lives, weak Christians are forced to take note. They will have before them a model who demonstrates that it is possible for a person to be totally committed to Christ. Then it is up to these weak Christians to decide whether or not to take the call to total commitment seriously.

2. Reputation with Non-Christians (3:7). Paul's second social qualification was that a prospective leader "must have a good reputation with outsiders, so that he will not fall into disgrace and into the devil's trap" (3:7). "Outsiders" here refers to non-Christians. The word rendered "reputation" *(marturia)* is usually translated "witness" or "testimony." A leader's behavior must stand out as something unusual, and people will take note of it. A leader's non-Christian neighbors, for example, should know him as honest, hardworking, always ready to help, and as one who regards rich and poor with equal respect and concern.

If Christian leaders fail to have a good testimony they "fall into disgrace and into the devil's trap." Satan makes full use of the fall that he himself has had a part in engineering. He is able to discredit not only the leader but also the cause which the leader represents. Outsiders observing the failure infer that Christianity is an impractical religion. When they are challenged to commit their lives to Christ, they say they do not need Christianity because it has no power to significantly change people's lives. They say Christianity is no different from their own powerless religion, so there is no need to go through the bother of changing religions.

Today we see many examples that add weight to the charge that Christianity is powerless to change lives. Many people in public life are testifying to God's blessings upon their lives. Some of them have risen to positions of leadership in the church. But some of them tell an occasional lie. Or they are not conscientious workers. Or they resort to unscrupulous business practices. Or they don't treat the poor with respect. They testify to the blessings of Christ, but don't exemplify the ethics of Christ. Unbelievers conclude that the grace of which these people speak is a cheap refuge for weak people who want to grab blessings for selfish gain, but who won't shoulder the responsibility of living a righteous life. Christianity, as a result, is discredited in the eyes of unbelievers.

A leader who practices what he preaches provokes an unbeliever to consider Christ. The unbeliever will be compelled to admit that there is a power in Christianity that helps people to live according to their principles. This strikes a chord of hope in a person who has become weary of having to break his principles in order to survive in an evil society. A thirst is created in him for a more authentic kind of life. And the Christian's God seems to promise such a life to him. Right living opens the door for an effective witness. Because this is true, we can see how important a good reputation is for Christian leaders. A bad reputation would be one obvious reason for disqualifying a person from leadership.

If one who is already a leader is guilty of a sin that significantly tarnishes his reputation, he should have to be removed from office, even if he has repented of this sin. He must be kept on in the fellowship and ministered to lovingly. But he cannot return to leadership until he has clearly given evidence of the fruit of repentance (Matt. 3:8). Without this fruit he will not be able to retrieve his reputation.

ABILITY TO TEACH (3:2)

Notice that the only ministry-related qualification for an overseer in Paul's list is that the prospective leader "must be . . . able to teach" (3:2). This fact is not surprising in the light of our understanding of leadership as parenthood. One of the chief duties of parents is to feed their children. Similarly a Christian leader must feed those in his care with God's truth. His task is to lead God's people to a realization of God's will for them as a group and as individuals. The primary means through which this is done is teaching. So it is not surprising that there are many references to the teaching ministry in 1 Timothy (2:7; 3:2; 4:6, 11, 13; 5:17; 6:1, 3).

There may perhaps be some in the church with a special gift of teaching. Those people can specialize in teaching. Yet we cannot expect them to fulfill totally the need for teaching in the church. All leaders will need to do some teaching as one of the primary responsibilities of their leadership role. If they cannot teach, or will not teach, they shouldn't be put into positions of leadership.

We must hasten to add that the ability to teach is not a natural talent with which one is born. Teaching is a skill that all leaders can develop through adequate preparation. Of course some will do it better than others. But all leaders who work at it can do it with some degree of proficiency.

Paul gave a good description of the teaching ministry in his list of qualifications for elders in Titus. He said that an elder "must hold firmly to the trustworthy message as it had been taught" (1:9). Applying this in the twentieth century, we can affirm that an elder must be a person of the Word. Today, it is in the Scriptures that we find "the trustworthy message as it had been taught." A good leader knows the content of Scripture. He has learned how to study the Scriptures and how to use them for his life and ministry. Paul said elsewhere that he did his "best to present [himself] to God as one approved, a workman who does not need to be ashamed and who correctly handles the word of truth" (2 Tim. 2:15).

If one is to hold firmly to the teaching he must be convinced of the truth of the message. Liberalism, which invaded the church in this century, could not produce this type of leader. It left the church with no clear message from God. The Bible affirms that God has spoken a definite word to man. Liberalism left us without any assurance of what that word was. As a result, doctrinal teaching went out of fashion in the church. In its place came discussions on current affairs, which carried none of the authority that belongs to the proclamation of the Word of God. A generation grew up ignorant of God's Word and of his ways.

Paul said that by holding firm to the teaching, an elder would "be able to encourage others by sound doctrine" (Titus 1:9). The knowledge of Scripture gives a foundation for the communication of doctrine. Today the practice of instruction in sound doctrine has fallen into disrepute for reasons other than liberalism. Many Christians associate this practice with correct ("sound"), but boring and irrelevant discourses. Sometimes when church members describe a person as a teacher, they are also implying that he is not a good communicator. "Don't use him for a Sunday service," they say. "He's a teacher, not a preacher." But the Sunday service is the most important place for feeding the flock with God's truth. Our point here is that teachers must work on developing communication skills.

How can a teacher communicate truth in a lively fashion? The first requirement is that the reality of the message should first be experienced in the teacher's own life. If so, what comes out is not merely an orthodox exposition of truth but a glad proclamation of life-transforming realities by a transformed person. Even the artistry of a brilliant communicator will have a hollow ring to it if the prerequisite of life-transformation has not been met.

A lively communicator also gives attention to how he can most effectively present his material to the audience he is seeking to teach. He chooses words they understand, illustrations with which they can identify, and applications that are relevant to their lives. He seeks to arrive at a proper balance between the practical and the theoretical. He arrives at the most suitable sequence in which to present his material. These qualities are only achieved when one gives himself to careful preparation.

The third characteristic of a good teacher is the ability to "refute those who oppose" sound doctrine (Titus 1:9). He knows the false doctrines to which those under his care are being exposed. And he is skilled in showing what is wrong with them.

PERSONAL APPLICATION

Give reasons why you are excited about Christian service. Then list the major problems you face in your ministry. Have the problems overshadowed your excitement over the ministry? If so, how can you remedy this situation?

FIVE
A LEADER'S BEHAVIOR (3:2, 3)

Eight of Paul's qualifications for an overseer have to do with the character and behavior of the leader. All of them seem to have some relationship to the person's ability to control himself when under pressure. The pressure may come from different sources such as adverse circumstances, temptation, or difficult people.

We cannot assess a person's character properly until we have seen him under pressure. A person may do very well at an interview or fill out an application in a very impressive manner. But these don't give any indication of how he will react when things get difficult. And it is under such circumstances that leadership is really put to the test.

A GOOD LEADER IS TEMPERATE (3:2)

The first behavior qualification we discuss is temperance. The word used here was formerly used in connection with strong drink. But later on it took on the meaning of temperate or sober. A leader must be one who exercises moderation. He knows when to stop.

A temperate person enjoys life, but knows that his enjoyment is limited by concern for others. So he won't, for example, disturb his neighbors with loud parties at night and he won't spend hours at a club at cost to his family. He advises people, but he knows also when to listen. He rebukes people, but knows when rebuke should end and encouragement begin. He encourages people, but knows when encouragement needs to give way to rebuke.

This quality in a person, like many of the others in Paul's list, grows with practice. Most people are not born temperate. But if a person works at acquiring this quality, with God's help it will gradually become second nature to him. This change is part of the process of maturing. A person who works on developing this quality would need to accept responsibility each time he fails to be temperate. It would involve disciplining oneself to say "No" to the temptation to go on when it is time to stop. As we apply ourselves conscientiously in this way, we will find that temperance gradually becomes a part of our nature. Before a person is appointed to leadership he should have developed this quality to a relatively high extent.

A GOOD LEADER IS SELF-CONTROLLED (3:2)

Self-control is somewhat similar to temperance. The idea behind the word Paul used here is a sound mind or self-mastery. To the Greeks this word described someone with a disciplined state of mind, not impulsive, and not given to extremes. A self-controlled person does not overreact in a crisis.

A leader cannot afford to panic and act irrationally every time he faces a crisis. The stability of the group he leads depends to a great extent on his own stability. If he loses control of himself he could drag the whole group down with him.

After overreacting in a crisis a leader may sometimes attempt to justify his behavior by saying something like, "I couldn't help it. He was unfair. He got on my nerves." But the damage caused by losing control is so serious that such behavior cannot be excused.

Why do people lose control of themselves in a crisis? We have already described one cause in our discussion of temperance: The person may not have matured fully. And maturity is a quality that develops gradually.

People also lose control of themselves and overreact at times when a sensitive area in their life has been touched. Such a person should ask himself why he is so sensitive in that area, as it may indicate an unresolved personality problem.

A person may feel that others don't accept him because of a certain experience or weakness in his life. It is more likely, however, that such a person acts this way because he does not accept himself because of the weakness. Around his problem an emotional wound has developed that has not been healed. It is a sensitive spot, and when touched, the person overreacts.

Early in my ministry with Youth For Christ in Sri Lanka I went through such an experience. I had succeeded as director a giant of a Christian leader, Sam Sherrard, a man to whom I was deeply indebted for my spiritual nurture. But his leadership style was somewhat different than mine. His strong points were my weak points, especially in the area of administration. Naturally, during my first few years in this job, people constantly compared me with him. I often heard comments such as, "Sam did it this way." Those who said things like this were not necessarily criticizing me. But these statements affected me deeply because they had touched a sensitive area in my life—an area that exposed my weaknesses.

About two years after I had taken over this position, Sam Sherrard visited Sri Lanka. It seemed to me that my weaknesses were very much in view. We had one public rally with Sam and, due to bad planning, that meeting was a disaster. For a time the bad feeling about the meeting seemed to loom over me and cover many other things that would have given me cause for encouragement. My reaction was very irrational. A few days after the rally, at a staff meeting, I scolded my colleagues in a way completely unlike myself. Some were quite hurt by it. During these days I often kept talking about resigning from my position. A sensitive spot in my life had been touched, and I had lost control of myself.

When we sense that there are areas of hurt in our lives, we must immediately initiate a process of healing. Otherwise it will drag us down and make us ineffective as leaders. I believe a process of healing was gradually set in motion in my own life. I learned to accept my weaknesses and, more important, I learned to live with them. I learned to make allowance for my weaknesses by getting others to help me with what I could not do well. And I am still working on improving my skills in these weak areas.

People lose control of themselves in many different situations. But often there are root causes which lie behind the "eruptions." Those who have these problems must get at the causes and seek to eliminate them. For as long as such problems have a major influence on the way a person acts, that person is not ready for leadership.

A GOOD LEADER IS RESPECTABLE (3:2)

The next quality required of a leader is respectability. Today, when we refer to a person as being respectable, we often imply that he is a stuffy person, always correct, but also grave, prim, and proper, and in an unattractive way.

The idea of correctness is found in the word Paul used here. But it is not a stiff correctness, for this word also carries the idea of beauty. Paul was referring to a beautiful correctness. He was saying here that a leader must be well behaved, a person who can always be trusted to act in a wise and good way—a way that earns him the respect of others.

A respectable person knows how to give things to people without putting them under obligation to him. He knows how to make requests of people under him without insulting them. He knows how to handle a crisis without stooping to such shameful methods as revenge, mudslinging, and violence. When he is asked to speak, he does not use the opportunity to ride his favorite hobbyhorse. He can be trusted to keep his word. If he makes a promise, he somehow tries in every way to fulfill it. This quality of respectability is also one that is acquired through practice.

By now it should have become clear that anyone interested in leadership development should devote much attention to developing the character of a prospective leader according to Christian standards, a matter often overlooked in our leadership training programs.

A GOOD LEADER IS NOT GIVEN TO MUCH WINE (3:3)

A leader's self-control must be manifested in the way he eats and drinks too. Paul's next qualification was that he should "not [be] given to much wine." That is, he cannot be a heavy drinker.

In ancient times the water supplies were often inadequate and sometimes dangerous, so it is not surprising that wine was a popular drink in the biblical world. It was regarded in the Bible as something bringing cheer (Judg. 9:13), which could be enjoyed if taken responsibly. It was also regarded as a good medicine, as Paul told Timothy (1 Tim. 5:23; see also Luke 10:34). The rabbis often used a saying, "Wine is the greatest of all medicines; where wine is lacking, there drugs are necessary" (cited by A. C. Schultz in *Zondervan Pictorial Encyclopedia of the Bible*, V, p. 938).

Yet there are repeated warnings in the Bible about the misuse of wine and strong drink as in Proverbs 23:29-35. The shameful results of drunkenness are seen in the lives of Noah (Gen. 9:18-27) and Lot (Gen. 19:30-38). The writer of Proverbs said, "Wine is a mocker and beer a brawler; whoever is led astray by them is not wise" (20:1).

Paul's attitude to wine was in keeping with that of the rest of Scripture. It may be used responsibly. But irresponsible use is inexcusable, because it disqualifies a person from leadership.

Paul said in another place, "It is better not to eat meat or drink wine or to do anything else that will cause your brother to fall" (Rom. 14:21). Total abstinence may be advisable in most situations, where wine could be a hindrance to effective witness. In most Eastern countries, for example, it is probably better for Christians not to drink alcoholic beverages. We cannot demand this of all Christians as an absolute rule, for we have no scriptural warrant for that. Yet, a person who drinks alcoholic beverages generally cannot "have a good reputation with outsiders" (3:7), especially in Buddhist, Hindu, or Muslim environments. The practice could close the door for an effective witness.

Buddhism has a basic moral code, the *Pancha Sila* (five precepts), which is the least that is required of every Buddhist. One of the five precepts in this code is the command to abstain from distilled or fermented liquors that cause intoxication. One who takes such simply could not be regarded as a righteous man. I will never forget a Buddhist university student telling me one day, "You Christians brought three Bs to Sri Lanka. The Bible, the Baila [a Portuguese dance], and the Booze!" She was talking of the Portuguese colonists. It is significant that predominantly Christian (actually Roman Catholic) areas in Sri Lanka are known for drunkenness. While the Hindus have no universally binding rule against drinking alcoholic beverages, the Brahmins and respected Hindu leaders such as Mahatma Gandhi have taken a strong stand against it.

Islam prides itself in having destroyed the terrible "Christian" practice of taking strong drink in the areas they "conquered" from the Christians. Muslims have the strictest rules on alcohol, but in some Muslim countries the "intemperate" Christians alone are given permits to purchase strong drink. When a Muslim friend of mine started associating with Christians he was warned by his family members that he would end up as a drunkard. And, for a while, he did drink too much.

So it is advisable, especially for Christian leaders who live in non-Christian societies, to abstain totally from alcohol use.

A CHRISTIAN LEADER IS NOT VIOLENT (3:3)

The next quality literally means, "not a giver of blows." Paul could be referring here to people misbehaving at noisy parties, acting brutally under the influence of liquor, getting involved in brawls and the like. But it is unlikely that such people would be considered for leadership. Paul was more than likely talking about the kind of treatment an impatient church leader might be tempted to give to some stubborn member of the church.

Sometimes even conscientious people act in such a violent way when those under them go out of line. They don't take time to check up on what really happened and why it happened. They simply explode with what is supposed to be righteous anger.

Such violent reactions to people's errors are rarely constructive. They don't result in a person changing his ways. They often create resentment. Out of fear, the wrongdoer may behave well, but inside he will remain bitter and hurt.

A CHRISTIAN LEADER IS GENTLE (3:3)

Far from exploding in a crisis, a leader reacts with gentleness or patience. Christ himself is described as having this quality (2 Cor. 10:1). Paul told the Christians in Philippi, "Let your gentleness be evident to all" (Phil. 4:5). The word for gentleness is sometimes translated as "forbearance," which gives us some idea of what the Greek word really means.

Aristotle described this quality as that which corrects justice. R. C. Trench defined it as that which "rectifies and redresses the injustices of justice" (Synonyms of the New Testament). We saw above how plain justice could be hard and unreasonable. Christian justice has a gentle touch to it. A Christian leader does not ignore or excuse wrong. Rather, he deals with it in such a way that the wrongdoer is encouraged to repent and return to the loving warmth of Christian fellowship. Elsewhere Paul instructed Timothy to correct and rebuke "with great patience" (2 Tim. 4:2).

Leaders must always be known for being willing to listen to the explanations of those who have done wrong, to be receptive to the feelings of the weak and the erring, and to be actively working for the restoration of wrongdoers.

A CHRISTIAN LEADER IS NOT QUARRELSOME (3:3)

The seventh behavior qualification we study literally means "disinclined to fight." So it has often been translated as "peaceable" or "conciliatory." The last thing a conciliatory person wants is a battle. Sometimes battles are inevitable, but one resorts to them only after every attempt at peace has been made. And even then the battle is carried out "Christianly," not ignoring such Christian qualities as love, gentleness, and kindness.

A quarrelsome person, when faced with a problem, prefers confrontation to conversation. A discussion on baptism, for example, becomes a personal clash. Such a person, without first discussing a problem on a personal level, brings it up at a meeting or through a harsh letter written to the person concerned, or, worse, a letter written to a third party. Such a person uses this method because he would be uneasy about friendly conversation with people "on the other side" of an issue. The hostility he has developed is incompatible with such conversation.

Such hostility toward people "on the other side" is often a symptom of hostility toward life itself. A quarrelsome person does not trust others. He always feels he is being wronged. He thinks he must expose the wrongs of people, because people must not be trusted. Because of this attitude toward other people, he often gives bad interpretations to the sincere and good actions of other people. Such a person is always ready to start a quarrel.

Such hostility generally grows in a person through bad experiences. Someone in the past may have let him down. Or he may not have been shown real love and acceptance by others. Such experiences often make a person bitter. The memory of these experiences looms over him like a dark cloud, blocking the light of grace, so that he looks at life always with a frown.

The blood of Jesus Christ can cleanse us from all such bad memories, but we must first consciously open up these memories to God so that he can apply his healing balm on them. Most people prefer to bury these memories in their subconscious minds because it is too painful to face up to them, or because they are not willing to forgive those who have hurt them. If we allow it, God's grace is able to flood the innermost recesses of our lives. We become overwhelmed with gratitude to God for lifting us out of the depths we were in and for exposing us to his marvelous light. That light dispels all the darkness in our lives.

Hostility cannot coexist with such gratitude. When he is wronged by someone, a "graced" person may for a time be angry about it. But the anger cannot survive for long. Soon the light of grace shines through and dispels the darkness caused by man's evil. Then the "graced" person says that, in spite of man's evil, grace will superabound and turn the situation into something good. So he can look at life with a smile because he affirms that, because of grace, life has been good to him. Such a person would want the beauty he is experiencing to invade all his relationships too. He cannot be quarrelsome.

A CHRISTIAN LEADER IS NOT A LOVER OF MONEY (3:3)

The issues relating to Paul's eighth behavior qualification—not a lover of money—have been dealt with at greater length in the last two chapters of this book. So our discussion here is very brief.

The indiscreet use of money has caused the downfall of many a promising minister. If there is some doubt related to the financial dealings or attitudes of a prospective leader, a very rigorous investigation must be carried out before he is appointed to office. Christian leadership brings with it many occasions which could tempt him to financial abuses. Even an honest person who still suffers from a love for money could end up disgruntled in the ministry because he feels he isn't paid enough for his services. Such people must not be appointed to leadership. Leaders must have developed strict financial disciplines before they are appointed to leadership.

Paul's list of qualifications may prompt some leaders to resign from their positions of leadership. Actually no one can say that he has achieved complete mastery in any of the areas discussed in this chapter. Yet at a certain stage of his pilgrimage, a Christian would normally reach some level of maturity that would qualify him for some leadership responsibility in the body of Christ. As more

Christlikeness develops, so might his level of responsibilities.

If a person does not develop spiritually as was expected of him, he shouldn't be promoted. This principle must be adhered to even if the person concerned shows a mastery of the other skills required for ministry. Paul's list has shown us that the primary qualifications for leadership relate to spiritual character and not to ministerial skills.

This is not an easy principle to follow. Often skills put a person in the limelight. And people wonder why such a talented person is not made a leader. Further, in our society people are expected to climb to higher positions with time. Again people wonder why a person has not been elevated at the usual time. If the person is a paid Christian worker, then his salary must be increased to keep pace with economic inflation even if he is not given higher responsibilities. But he can be given the responsibilities of over-seership only when he exhibits a Christlike character.

PERSONAL APPLICATION

Under what type of provocation do you lose control of yourself and overreact? Could there be an unhealed hurt that causes this? What steps should you take to remedy this weakness?

SIX
THE LEADER'S
FAMILY LIFE (3:2, 4–6)

In all of the lists of the qualifications for Christian leadership in 1 Timothy and Titus, there are references to the family life of the leader. The Bible presents some important principles relating to Christian family life which Christian leaders must exemplify.

Three family-life qualifications are required of overseers. The statements are made about male leaders, but the principles that underlie them apply to female leaders also.

A CHRISTIAN LEADER IS HUSBAND OF ONE WIFE (3:2)

Paul's first family-life qualification was that a leader should be "the husband of but one wife." This statement can be interpreted in three different ways. Some take this to mean that a leader can have only one wife at a time. Since polygamy was common in the first century, monogamy would have been a relevant requirement for a leader in the New Testament church.

The statement could also mean that Paul was prohibiting second marriages for overseers, and some take it to apply even to marriage after the death of the first wife. The statement could also be a specific way of saying something more general, that is, that an overseer must set an example of the highest morality.

Whatever the specific meaning of the statement may be, Paul's general idea was that leaders must have higher moral principles than those of the society in which they were living. The marriage relationship was under heavy fire in the first century. Barclay says that in those days, "the happy marriage was the astonishing exception." Into such a society Christianity came with a belief in "the inviolability of the marriage bond and the sanctity of the Christian home" (William Barclay, *The Daily Study Bible; The Letters to Timothy, Titus and Philemon,* Westminster Press, 1960).

Marriage is under heavy fire today also. Christian leaders must demonstrate that Christianity has an answer to this problem. Yet divorce has hit even the parsonage in a big way. How careful we must be then to ensure that those appointed to leadership should have stable marriages that are free from unwholesome sexual associations!

Being a committed Christian does not automatically insulate one from marital problems or from the temptation to unfaithfulness. Friction is inevitable when two diverse personalities seek to experience oneness. Resolving problems in marriage may be a long hard process involving much pain, confrontation, and humility. A true Christian will go through these difficult experiences believing that the risen Lord will ultimately give victory and a deep union. For this reason, Christians still hold to the inviolability of marriage, even though today's society has rejected such an idea as impractical.

We live in an age of instant solutions, of tranquilizers and painkillers. We think that by our advances in learning and technology we can avoid pain and get most of the things we want quickly. Our society has forgotten how to suffer and to wait. When quick solutions to their marital problems are not in sight, many people choose to end their marriages. They regard the struggle toward reconciliation to be too painful and tedious a process to endure.

I believe the crisis in family life today is the symptom of a deeper problem—we have not learned to suffer. But suffering is woven into the fabric of life in a fallen world. If we are to live meaningfully here, we must learn how to suffer, and marriage is one of the best places to learn this. Christians have the courage to face this suffering because they believe that on the other side of the suffering there is victory. They have this assurance because they serve a risen Savior.

So when inquiring into the marital relationship of a prospective leader, our primary concern is not whether he is having problems or not. We want to know whether he is working through his problems in a Christian way. We know that if he perseveres, a solution is on the way, and out of the struggle will emerge a deep and joyous relationship as an affirmation to the world that it is indeed normal for a man to be "the husband of but one wife."

A CHRISTIAN LEADER IS HOSPITABLE (3:2)

The second family-life qualification for Christian leadership is hospitality. The word "hospitable" *(philoxenos)* literally means "a lover of strangers." Hospitality was an important feature of New Testament Christianity (Rom. 12:13; Titus 1:8; 1 Pet. 4:9; Acts 2:46). Christians traveling in the first century would have tried to avoid the pagan atmosphere of the public inns, which would have served food that had been offered to idols.

Hospitality can also play an important part in church life today. Traveling preachers, Christians needing encouragement and fellowship, and people with special needs for care and shelter can benefit from Christian hospitality. It may take the form of a single meal, or having people in the home for a few days, or what has been called "radical hospitality," which is having homeless or psychologically or spiritually needy people over for an extended period.

Yet today many Christians are reluctant to host others. An American pastor, Donald Bubna, surveyed many Christians to find reasons for this reluctance. The two main reasons he found were that having guests frightened some prospective hosts and that some felt their home furnishings were too modest or inadequate. Others said they were too busy, the expense of showing hospitality was too great, and the tension and exhaustion from getting the house cleaned and the food prepared was too much for them *(Building People through a Caring Sharing Fellowship,* Tyndale House, 1978).

Bubna points out that the most common reasons for the reluctance to host others stem from pride. He says, "To be ashamed of our furniture or afraid of serving an inadequate meal can best be described as pride." The same point is made by Karen Burton Mains in her excellent book on hospitality, *Open Heart—Open Home* (David C. Cook, 1976). She says, "True hospitality comes before pride." Hospitality has "nothing to do with impressing people, but everything to do with making them feel welcome and wanted."

Mrs. Mains is a pastor's wife. Many church activities were held in her home. She says that for some years it seemed as though she "did nothing but clean up after people." After each group left, she had to toil to get the house back into shape so that it would be ready for the next group. Yet she was not a housekeeper by nature. Sometimes she would delay cleaning up the house if company was not expected.

On one such day someone from the church came to visit her. The house was in a mess. Let Mrs. Mains tell what happened:

Hospitality before pride . . . I reminded myself dismally. Determined, I welcomed the woman with warmth, invited her into the unsightly rooms and refused to embarrass her with apologies. I consciously let go of my pride. [The visitor's response amazed her.] "I used to think you were perfect," she said, "but now I think we can be friends."

This story is not intended to provide an excuse for keeping an untidy house. Rather, it is to show that the key to hospitality is not our performance as housekeepers and cooks but our openhearted friendship which makes people feel welcome and wanted. The fellowship is the main thing. The food is secondary, as Jesus sought to show Martha when she entertained him at her home (Luke 10:38-42).

Mrs. Mains contrasts Christian hospitality with secular entertainment. She says, "Demanding perfection, fostering an urge to impress . . . is a rigorous task master which enslaves." Many people shy away from hospitality because they have confused it with entertainment.

Entertainment often results in disappointment over dishes that did not come out right, resentment over the extra work involved, neglected children, and family quarrels. We never seem to be able to perform as well as we want to. So there is disappointment and friction.

How important then it is for us to return to the practice of simple, informal, relaxed and friendly hosting! Some may criticize us for being frugal and unimaginative. But the joy of being a blessing to so many people far outweighs this unpleasantness.

Bubna makes another important observation about hospitality which we often overlook. He reminds us that in 1 Timothy and

Titus it is the man who is required to be hospitable—not just his wife. He says the husband "was meant to go beyond inviting the guests and then sitting in the living room to entertain them while [his wife] did the rest." Hospitality is an activity in which the whole family can play some part. The husband can get involved in deciding what food to prepare, in buying things for the meals, in cleaning up the house, and in washing up the dishes after it is all over. Both husband and wife need to be involved in the decision to invite someone, unless in the case of an emergency.

Sharing the work load takes away a lot of the wife's burden in hospitality. The experience also becomes an enjoyable part of sharing life together. Family life can lose a lot of its beauty if each member insists on doing his own projects independent of the others. Combined family projects deepen ties and bring a joyous freshness to the home.

A CHRISTIAN LEADER
MANAGES HIS FAMILY WELL (3:4, 5)

The third family-life qualification for a leader is that he, as head of the household, must ensure that it runs in an orderly manner. A family is mismanaged when there is neglect or unwise leadership.

A leader can neglect his family by being too busy in the pursuit of his career so that his wife has to bring up the children single-handedly. The unique role a father plays in the development of his children is missed, as he has shirked his responsibility as the head of the home.

It is not easy for one who strives for excellence in his career to devote time and energy to the home. Career related projects often have urgent deadlines. The measurable results coming from these projects are often regarded as a gauge of the leader's suitability for his job, so he "must" perform. Such "urgent" pressure could tyrannize a person to the point where he is neglecting routine family responsibilities. This has been called the "tyranny of the urgent." We break this tyranny by deliberately exerting ourselves to give priority to the "routine."

Take the example of a leader who comes home after completing a difficult project which demanded his full effort. He is physically tired and emotionally drained. He would like to relax. It is not a time when he is naturally inclined to give attention to the affairs of the family. But while he was away his wife had toiled alone to keep the house running smoothly. The children had missed their father. They need attention. But only by exerting himself could a tired person give such attention. Yet a well-managed home is the reward of just such exertion.

The other reason for mismanagement of the home is unwise leadership. Some parents, for example, are too strict or over-protective. They give little opportunity to their family members for creative expression, for growth in maturity, and for the joyous freedom that ought to be a part of the Christian life. Other parents are too lenient. They overlook faults or don't regard them as seriously as they should. Direction, correction, and discipline are necessary for a child to grow up in a healthy fashion.

A good manager not only spends time with his family but also spends the time wisely. He corrects, but also compliments and encourages. He works and plays with his family members. He plans and prays with them. He weeps and laughs with them. His strength, his talents, his humor and his creativity are not just expended on his career but are also used effectively in the home.

Paul went on to give the consequence of good management of the home: "His children obey him with proper respect." Paul was not saying that the leader's children need to be believers, though this is the highest blessing that one could wish for a child. The decision to commit one's life to Jesus Christ is, however, a personal choice that people make individually. The father is not ultimately responsible for it. Paul's point was that the father's behavior should be such that his leadership is accepted by his children. So they "obey" or, more literally, "submit" to him.

The expression, "with proper respect," could apply either to the father or to the children. If it applies to the father it means that he should be dignified in the way he behaves. If to the children, it means they should regard their father with proper respect. The two ideas are related, for children will not respect a father who behaves in an undignified manner.

Hendriksen catches the sense of this verse well: "The authority must be exercised . . . in such a manner that the father's firmness makes it advisable for a child to obey, that his wisdom makes it natural for a child to obey, and that his love makes it a pleasure for a child to obey" (William Hendriksen, *The New Testament Commentary, I & II Timothy and Titus,* Edinburgh: The Banner of Truth Trust, 1960).

Verse 5 gives the reason why Paul made proper management of the house a necessary qualification for leadership. He said, "If anyone does not know how to manage his own family, how can he take care of God's church?" Christian leadership essentially has to do with relationships. One's family is the group of people to whom he relates most intimately. If he can't relate to this group properly, it means he is not fully competent in handling interpersonal relationships. If he isn't, he does not qualify for the leadership of God's people.

A CHRISTIAN LEADER
IS NOT A RECENT CONVERT (3:6)

The word translated "recent convert" *(neophutos),* from which we get the word *neophyte,* literally means "newly planted." It was used in a literal sense of newly planted trees. The roots of such trees have not yet been established. One who leads God's people must be "rooted and built up in" Christ (Col. 2:6). In order to lead people effectively in the ways of God, the leader must himself first be established in these ways. Through consistent practice, the "ways of God" should become second nature to him, a characteristic that takes time to develop.

Sometimes we encounter new converts whom we recognize as "born leaders." Even before their conversion they possess some qualifications for leadership. But these must not be confused with spiritual maturity, which comes from extended exposure to God and his Word.

Further, the ministry can be compared to a long distance steeplechase rather than to a sprint, a run that brings with it challenges that can sap our energies. To persevere amidst these challenges one must have learned endurance. We need endurance to labor on in hope when no fruit appears to be on the way, endurance to live with the non-ideal, to keep our head in the midst of a crisis. This type of endurance grows slowly, often in the school of hard knocks, as both Paul and James have shown (Rom. 5:3; James 1:2-4). New converts generally abound with enthusiasm, but it does not mean they have the endurance required for the demands of leadership. Yet people are often wrongly elevated to leadership solely on the merits of their enthusiasm.

Next Paul described what could happen if a recent convert is put into leadership: "He may become conceited and fall under the same judgment as the devil." Satan also had leadership opportunities, but he fell into the sin of pride and opened himself to severe judgment. Such could be the fate of an unprepared person who is suddenly elevated to leadership.

The verb translated "become conceited" literally means, "to wrap in smoke" or "becloud." Such a person cannot perceive things properly. Such a person thinks he has arrived. He is not on guard against temptation, and even though he thinks he is standing firm, he is quite liable to fall (1 Cor. 10:12). There is no one to warn him or discipline him since, after all, he is now a leader. If someone corrects him, he thinks, "Perhaps he is finding fault with me because he is jealous of my position." The stage is set for a big fall. And the fall is all the more serious because when a leader falls, the dishonor to Christ is compounded.

Many privileges and powers come with leadership which a proud person doesn't often handle well without abusing. He has authority over other people and can use them to fulfill his own ends. He has opportunity to push his name forward and to boost his ego. He has power to crush people who resist him. He has the freedom to schedule his time as he wishes. All these are dangerous weapons in the hands of a conceited person.

And then there is the praise, which is one of the occupational hazards of Christian ministry. Ministers are often put in the limelight. People will flatter them, especially if they are good orators and have an attractive public presence. Some people confuse these personality traits with spirituality and godliness. Only a soundly rooted person can handle the challenge that comes from such praise. Often, because they are "beclouded," they believe these inaccurate words of praise said about them. They could ride on the praise, neglecting other key areas of their lives, such as financial accountability, Bible study and prayer, accountability to the body of Christ, and family responsibility.

One of the best antidotes to the ill effects of flattery is a close, open relationship with a few believers and with our family members. They know who we really are and will love us enough to burst some of the unrealistic bubbles we have built up around ourselves. Many conceited people, however, avoid such "ego-deflating" relationships. Paul was obviously very wise in giving this caution about appointing new converts to leadership.

How do we know when a person is ready for leadership? The answer varies with the person and the situation. Unusually gifted and dedicated people may be put into leadership roles in a shorter time than others. In a completely new Christian community, leadership may be given earlier than in an established community such as in Ephesus, where Timothy served. So when writing to Titus, serving the newer church in Crete, Paul left out this requirement for leadership. Of course this brings with it a more exacting responsibility to gauge carefully a person's commitment to Christ and suitability for leadership.

Leroy Eims has suggested a seven-year training period after conversion before a person is given leadership. Seven years does seem like a long period, but Eims points out that it took three years of concentrated attention before Christ had prepared his disciples for leadership. They would have been exposed to him for about twelve hours a day over this period. This would amount to 13,140 hours, much more time than a discipler is usually able to spend with a trainee *(The Lost Art of Disciple Making,* Zondervan, 1978). And most of us don't do any leadership training of the type that Christ did. We just expect leaders to emerge from our churches, and complain when they don't.

A seven-year time frame for leadership development does not imply that the growing Christian must be inactive for seven years. Oswald Sanders has some good advice: "The promising convert should be afforded a widening opportunity to serve at humbler and less prominent tasks that would develop both natural and spiritual gifts." Sanders summarizes by saying, "He should not be advanced too fast, lest he becomes puffed up. Neither should he be repressed, lest he be discouraged" *(Spiritual Leadership,* London: Lakeland, 1967).

In our study of Paul's list of qualifications for leadership, we looked at social qualifications dealing with a person's reputation. We saw many behavior qualifications related to a person's ability to live a controlled life. We saw one ministry qualification—the aptitude to teach. We saw three family-life qualifications and one qualification relating to spiritual maturity. All of these have underscored the importance of being careful in choosing leaders.

PERSONAL APPLICATION

As you went through this lesson, some ideas would have come into your mind about how you could enrich your family life. Write these down.

SEVEN
HOW TO RESPOND
TO FALSE TEACHING (4:1–6)

The false teaching which Timothy faced in Ephesus was constantly in Paul's mind when he wrote to him (1:3-11, 19, 20; 4:1-16; 6:3-5, 20, 21). Earlier in this epistle, Paul reminded Timothy that he had been kept on in Ephesus so that he could combat this teaching (1:3). Paul gave him a model of how a leader, then and now, should respond to false teaching (4:1-8). The heresies we encounter today may be different, but there is much that we can learn from this passage.

THE TEACHING EXPOSED (4:1-3a)

With his characteristic unaccommodating attitude to error, Paul exposed this false teaching in verses 1-3a. We note that Paul had done his "homework" of finding out what was being taught and who was teaching it. He was able to use this information in formulating his response to the teaching.

One of the first steps in responding to erroneous teaching, therefore, is to gain a knowledge of its contents. If we try to oppose error without the facts, our opponents would be able to discredit our case by saying something like, "Don't take him seriously. He doesn't even know what he is talking about." Most of us already know that active members of cults have been well trained with facts about their teachings and the questions that people will ask about them. Christians not fully grounded in the

Word are often impressed by this knowledge. So, we too will have to be armed with facts if we are to counter the false teachings.

A Predicted Heresy (4:1a). Paul first said that the apostasy had been predicted: "The Spirit clearly says that in later times some will abandon the faith" (4:1a). When Timothy saw the initial growth of the heresy, he may have been tempted to panic. But Paul wanted to reassure Timothy by reminding him that God knew what was happening. In fact, he had foreseen it and predicted it. The knowledge of this was given through a specific prophecy, the details of which are not known to us.

The fact that God knows all about what is happening is a great resource to us for any battle we carry out. For a time a demon-inspired error may seem to have great power. But we know that God is sovereign, and his purposes will be ultimately fulfilled. We are not fighting a losing battle. God had anticipated this deviation from truth and made plans for its defeat, which means that we are on the winning side. We do not approach the battle with an insecure defensiveness, but with an attitude of confidence and authority.

Feeling insecure and defensive won't help us in the battle for truth. It may win arguments, but it rarely wins people to the side of truth. Thinking people sense the apologist's restlessness. They are repelled by the insensitive authoritarian attitude that goes along with the defensiveness. When we place our confidence in God, we also speak with authority. We are dogmatic about the truth. But ours is a controlled dogmatism that is willing to reason intelligently on behalf of truth. Such an approach would do much more to encourage thinking people to change their minds and accept the truth.

It was with this confidence in God that Paul approached heresy in this passage. Paul was not writing like a frightened person. He had the authority of a confident proclaimer, of an ambassador of the King of kings.

Its Origin and Its Teachers (4:1b, 2). Paul's dogmatism was evidenced in verses 1b and 2 as he forthrightly exposed the origin of the heresy and those who teach it. The origin, he said, was demonic. So those who accept the heresy "follow deceiving spirits and things taught by demons" (4:1b). The teachers are "hypocritical liars, whose consciences have been seared as with a hot iron"

(4:2). They speak as if they present the truth. But their minds are so hardened and closed up that they are unable even to be penetrated by the truth.

Today many of us are reluctant to speak with the forthrightness we see here. We say people must be given the freedom to think and express themselves in any way they wish. We pride ourselves about having a pluralistic church that leaves room for divergences of opinion. Anyone who is against such pluralism is charged with being too exclusive or narrow. But those who are committed to scriptural Christianity agree that there is an essential, unchanging body of truth which constitutes the historic faith of the church from which no deviations can be accommodated.

Are we, then, advocating a dead orthodoxy? We are advocating an orthodoxy in the sense that all Christian thinking should be controlled by the boundaries set by the Scriptures. The biblical Christian believes that God has spoken a definite Word to man and that this Word is not only the foundation for all his thinking, but that it also sets the boundaries within which he confines his thinking. The biblical Christian humbly acknowledges that the God who created this world and set it in motion knew how men could best achieve authenticity and fulfillment on earth, and that with this knowledge God has given man a complete and sufficient revelation. This revelation becomes man's canon—his rule or standard—for thought and action.

Yet by committing ourselves to a completed revelation we are not automatically condemning ourselves to a dead orthodoxy. Contained in this revelation are treasures which are so vast that after centuries of theological discovery our task is still unfinished. Besides, each age brings with it the challenge to communicate the unchanging truth in a way that is both relevant and understandable to contemporary man. So, theology must always be alive, constantly expressing itself in new forms.

In fact, for theology to be truly Christian, it must be creative. Man is made in the image of a God who is creative. To be like God, then, is to be creative. Philip Hughes summarizes our position well:

The creative task of theology must be performed with the given "material" of the Word of God written, from whose pages the same Holy Spirit causes the truth to beam forth with inexhaustible wonder and beauty, so that it is always an unfinished task, and always a task with limitless possibilities ahead. (Creative Minds in Contemporary Theology, *Eerdmans, 1969.)*

So a plurality of expression and understanding within the church is a sign of health, a sign of the freshness that comes from the use of God's gift of creativity. But each of these expressions needs to spring from and be bounded by the Word of God. If they veer from this Word, they lead people away from an authentic existence and are thus damaging to them. They must be roundly condemned, not only in the interests of truth (we are not just "heresy hunters"), but also because of our concern for the welfare of people. So the defense of orthodoxy, with its accompanying condemnation of heterodoxy, is ultimately an expression of love—love for the truth and its source, God, and love for mankind.

Its Contents (4:3). Paul presented a key feature of the heresy Timothy was encountering: "They forbid people to marry and order them to abstain from certain foods" (v. 3a). The false teachers were advocating asceticism as a necessary condition for true spirituality.

Asceticism appeals to certain Christians who are troubled by their failures in the spiritual life. They are looking for something extra which they can do to speed their growth in godliness. Asceticism seems to provide an answer to this quest. The struggling Christian reasons that it is because of desires for earthly things, such as sex, food, and clothing, that he keeps falling into sin. So, he tries to do away with these evil desires and join that superior band of Christians who have chosen to go "all the way" in their commitment to Christ.

WHY IT IS WRONG (4:3b-5)

After exposing the false teaching, Paul then used a theological argument to show why it was wrong. Ours is a reasonable faith, so the truthfulness of the beliefs to which we adhere can be demonstrated. We can know why we believe. Knowing not only the "what" of belief but also the "why" makes a person's faith strong, and equips him to weather challenges to his faith. Therefore, it is a leader's responsibility to teach both the what and the why of belief.

Asceticism versus Creationism. Paul argued that asceticism was incompatible with the doctrine of creation (4:3b-5). He said that these foods, which the false teachers prohibit, were "created [by God] to be received with thanksgiving by those who believe and know the truth" (4:3b). He continued: "For everything God created is good, and nothing is to be rejected if it is received with thanksgiving" (4:4). The ascetics tell us to stop enjoying earthly pleasures because they are hindrances to spirituality. The doctrine of creation tells us that earthly pleasures are gifts from God to be enjoyed with thanksgiving.

The ascetics would say, for example, that marriage is a concession introduced to ensure the perpetuation of the human race and to provide an avenue for the normal fleshly urges for sex and companionship. The higher you go in the spiritual life, they would say, the less you need to fulfill these urges, and with maturity, you must give them up entirely. The doctrine of creation tells us that marriage is part of God's beautiful plan for man. Sex and companionship are beautiful gifts intended to be enjoyed with thanksgiving, even by the most deeply spiritual people.

To the ascetic, Christianity is essentially a spiritual religion. To the biblical Christian, Christianity is a religion for all of life. It includes the spiritual, but it also includes the physical and emotional sides of life. God created all of these when he created life.

In the next verse Paul said that the material gift of God is legitimate "because it is consecrated by the word of God and prayer" (4:5). The ascetic says we must destroy the flesh. The hedonist says we must indulge the flesh, so he dedicates himself to the pursuit of pleasure even at the cost of his principles. The biblical Christian says we must consecrate the flesh by "the word of God and prayer." The word "consecrated" *(hagiazetai)* means "made holy." To consecrate the flesh is to surrender it to God and let him direct us into using it according to his will. The flesh becomes a means of fulfilling the will of God, which is the best way to use the flesh, for the will of God is "good, pleasing and perfect" (Rom. 12:2).

Paul said that God's gift is "consecrated by . . . prayer," which means that prayer should accompany our use of God's physical gifts. We say grace before meals—a practice which Jesus followed, but which many "enlightened" Christians today, for some strange reason, consider unimportant! Our wedding ceremonies are constantly punctuated by prayer. Prayer should even be a part of the sex act, for God has made this act holy. In our enjoyment of this deep expression of marital communion, we also concurrently enjoy communion with God. The threefold cord of marriage remains threefold during the sex act too.

The expression "by the word of God" is also used in connection with consecration. It may mean that the consecrated use of God's gifts always accords with what is taught in the Word of God. Or it may mean that the prayers of consecration offered when these gifts are used contain the words of Scripture. In the early church, prayers said before meals and at marriage ceremonies were saturated with quotations from Scripture.

The Importance of the Doctrine of Creation. This passage reminds us of how important the doctrine of creation is in Christian thinking. References to creation appear many times in the Scriptures. The creation was the starting point of all the major creeds of the church. So we would expect creation to be a key topic in Christian teaching. We would expect it to figure prominently in our follow-up courses for new converts. But it seems that the only time creation surfaces in our instruction today is when discussing the challenges the doctrine faces from those who hold to the theory of evolution.

The doctrine of creation is particularly important today as it clearly contradicts many of the non-Christian ideologies a Christian encounters today. The Bible says that God created the world. Naturalistic evolution says the world evolved by chance. The Bible says that God is distinct from his creation. Hindu pantheistic monism says that the world is an extension of the divine and is essentially one with it and salvation *(moksha)* is achieved when one loses his individuality and becomes one with the godhead.

Biblical Christianity affirms that creation is a material reality. The Hindu concept of *Maya* looks at the material in terms of an illusion.

Biblical Christianity says that God made life, as we experience it today, as something good, and earthly things are to be enjoyed through consecration. Asceticism says the earthly is bad and must be destroyed.

Because the earthly is good, Christians see salvation in terms of redemption—redemption of the created order, redemption through transformation of man's desires and humanness. Buddhism views the present existence on earth in terms of suffering. Thus, salvation (Nirvana) is viewed in terms of a completely different type of existence to life as we know it, an existence where desire is annihilated.

Biblical Christianity says man is a spiritual being, made in the image of God, a being who will be complete only as he relates favorably with God. Materialism, including atheistic Communism, says the only category that is of significance to man is what relates to this world.

Biblical Christianity says God gave man the responsibility to look after this world. So, the Christian gets involved conscientiously in the affairs of the world. Isolationism says that only the next world is important, and while he is on earth man has simply got to "hold the fort" waiting until the end comes.

Because man has the responsibility to look after this world, the biblical Christian seeks to conserve the earth's resources and so advocates ecological responsibility. Selfish people denude the earth of its resources and pollute its atmosphere. They are in danger of leaving behind an unlivable world for succeeding generations.

Because of these wrong views, we need to reintroduce creation into the church's curriculum. I would suggest the first two chapters of Genesis as a basic resource, since all the biblical affirmations about creation given above are derived from this passage.

GUIDING MEMBERS AMIDST HERESY (4:6a)

We have just studied how Paul guided Timothy on the response he should make towards the false teaching in the church (4:1-5). We saw how it was a model of good teaching. Paul told Timothy to guide the members of his congregation in the same way. He said, "If you point these things out to the brothers you will be a good minister of Jesus Christ" (4:6a). A good minister is a teacher, one who equips believers with truth so that they can handle the challenges they face.

The word translated "point . . . out" is not a strong word. It has the idea of "suggest," and the verse is elsewhere translated as, "Put these instructions before the brethren." The Greek word used here literally means, "to place under." Timothy was to place before the believers these truths so that they become like stepping stones upon which a person could traverse on treacherous ground. The task of the teacher is not simply to spoonfeed Christians by always telling them what to do. Rather, he placed truth before them so that they could use it to walk in faithfulness, while other misleading voices constantly clamored for their attention.

This fact must not be taken to mean that the teacher can never speak with authority and offer definite guidance to those in his care. Paul made this clear a little later by giving the other side of the teaching ministry: "Command and teach these things" (4:11). This word "command" is a strong one with military overtones and implies that Timothy must speak authoritatively. As one who communicates the authoritative truth of God, the teacher has the responsibility to insist among the faithful that God's way be followed. But he must know when to insist and when to suggest.

NOURISHMENT FOR THE TEACHER (4:6c)

The first part of verse 6 presents the output side of a teaching ministry. The second part presents the intake side. A good minister is "brought up in the truths of the faith and the good teaching that [he has] followed."

The statement, "truths of the faith and the good teaching [or doctrine]" refers to that body of teaching which was passed on by the apostles and which formed the foundation of Christian belief in Timothy's time. Timothy received these truths directly from Paul himself. Today we have these truths recorded in Scripture.

Timothy is said to have been "brought up" or, more literally, nourished on these truths. This verb is in the present tense pointing to a continuous process. *The Amplified Bible* renders it "ever nourishing your own self on the truths of the faith." Paul was saying that Timothy must feed upon the truths of the gospel daily, for that is how a mature Christian leader like Timothy will keep on growing and remain fresh in the ministry.

It is common to see Christian leaders who once were on fire for the Lord and active in his service now existing without the zeal of the early years. Some are not involved in Christian service at all. Others are doing it in an unenthusiastic, mechanical fashion. They are burned out, suffering from spiritual exhaustion, and without energy left for zealous service. Is this common phenomenon excusable? Most certainly not! The Bible describes the normal Christian life as a progression in maturity and in the warmth of commitment.

Why then do people burn out or grow stale? Often it is because during their years of active, zealous service they neglected one or more of the vital elements of the Christian life. One element commonly neglected is the devotional life. Such people had been so busy serving God that they had no time for unhurried times alone with God and his Word. They did not take in adequate spiritual nourishment, and spiritual emptiness is the outcome of this lack of nourishment. They have nothing more to give, so they either drop out of service or go through the routine of Christian activity with no zeal or effectiveness.

Spiritual malnutrition is not easy to diagnose until in its advanced stages. If a person is active in Christian service, we automatically regard him as being spiritually healthy. Yet this very activity, which we have taken as a sign of health, may be carried out in such a way as to cause ill health. One of the most absorbing challenges a Christian worker faces is the challenge to balance the output side of his life with the intake side; his service with his worship.

George Mueller was a person who, despite a hectic life of ministry, was able to maintain his freshness over an amazingly long period of time. At age seventy, after almost fifty years of preaching, and after establishing orphanages for thousands of destitute children, he launched out on an itinerant ministry. For seventeen more years he traveled with his wife, visiting forty-two countries and preaching to an estimated three million people. One reason he has given for his remarkable preservation is "love he felt for the Scriptures, and the constant recuperative power they exercised upon his whole being" (Basil Miller, *George Mueller: Man of Faith*, Bethany House, 1972). Mueller found the Scriptures had recuperative power. They were an antidote to burnout.

I have heard veteran Christian leaders describe how they spent hours poring over the Scriptures during their early years as Christians. They claim that those times of study gave them the foundation for their present ministry. Certainly it is essential for new Christians to immerse themselves in the Word. But there is no warrant for reducing the intensity of their study of the Word once they mature. I fear some of the veteran leaders referred to above seemed to imply this as they talked of those early years of Bible study.

Now some mature Christians may say that because they have gone through the Scriptures many times they do not need to go through the same material over again. Yet there are many reasons why even a mature Christian needs to go through the Scriptures regularly, many times over.

First, however mature we are and however well we know the Scriptures, we still continue to face challenges to our commitment from the world around us, and from our own sinful nature. The world continues to bombard us with principles and values which are opposed to the way of the Cross. We can drift into accepting these values without realizing it. For example, we may come to regard success in purely material terms, the way the world does, and forget that in God's kingdom success is measured by faithfulness to God's will. Because of such dangers, our thinking needs to be constantly challenged by a corresponding exposure to the principles and values of God as found in His Word.

A second reason for mature Christians to go through the Scriptures regularly is that one could never say on earth that he knows all of Scripture. There are inexhaustible riches in God's Word, the depths of which we could never plumb and the heights of which we could never attain to in this life. As we read and reread portions with open hearts and minds, more and more riches are opened to us. Familiar passages which we may know from memory suddenly come alive with new freshness as God reveals to us a facet of the truths they contain which we had not hitherto discovered.

Third, even though we may have a near perfect knowledge of the facts of Scripture, none of us perfectly adheres to these facts in our own lives. I've memorized that great "love chapter," 1 Corinthians 13, and preached many sermons and taught many studies from it. But each time I study it, I am convicted of my failure to live up to its teachings. So as long as we say with Paul, "I have not attained" (cf. Phil. 3:12, 13), we need to hear God speak to us from his Word urging us on along the path to perfection.

We are not surprised, then, when we read of Paul asking the veteran Timothy to regularly nourish himself in the Word. Neither are we surprised when we read that God told the veteran Joshua,

"Do not let this Book of the Law depart from your mouth; meditate on it day and night, so that you may be careful to do everything written in it" (Josh. 1:8). Joshua must have already had a mastery of the Book of the Law. But still he needed to meditate on it day and night. So we too need to find a means by which we are constantly exposed to the totality of God's Word.

Our first step would be to apportion time daily for unhurried moments with God and his Word. If we do not get into a disciplined routine of Bible reading, we will soon find that we are not doing it with any degree of regularity.

I believe one of the most alarming signs of ill health in the modern evangelical movement is that many of its leaders are not studying the Scriptures daily. Many say they don't have time for long seasons of wrestling with the Word. Some content themselves with a little "devotional" from an inspirational book of daily readings. They can't find time for anything more involved because they are too busy doing "God's work."

If a leader cannot find time for unhurried fellowship with God and his Word because he is too busy, there must be an element of disobedience in that busyness. He must reorder his priorities if he is to avert spiritual ruin. He should either change this situation or be removed from leadership responsibilities.

The next step is to choose a scheme by which we can go through the whole Bible in a certain time span. Numerous schemes are available for going through the Bible in a year. This has been a practice of many great servants of God through the centuries and has been recently advocated by John Stott and Martyn Lloyd-Jones in their outstanding books on preaching (Stott, *I Believe in Preaching,* London, Hodder & Stoughton, 1982); (Lloyd-Jones, *Preaching and Preachers,* Zondervan, 1972). Both Stott and Lloyd-Jones recommend Robert Murray McCheyne's "Bible Reading Calendar" (available through the Banner of Truth Trust, 3 Murrayfield Road, Edinburgh, Scotland). The popular guide, *Search the Scriptures,* takes the reader through the Bible in three years. You may evolve your own scheme, as many have done.

It is necessary for a Christian to go through the whole Bible because the different parts of Scripture have emphases unique to them, and we need to be exposed to each of these emphases if we are to think as God does. Many today neglect the study of the Old Testament, even though its message is particularly relevant to contemporary society. So the reading scheme we choose should ensure that we are constantly exposed to the different parts of Scripture (the Law, History, Wisdom literature, the Prophets, the Gospels, Acts, the Epistles, and Revelation).

Paul concluded by saying that Timothy had "followed the good teaching" (v. 6). Donald Guthrie says that this could either mean that he had closely investigated this teaching or that he had followed the teaching as a standard *(The Pastoral Epistles,* London: Tyndale Press, 1957). Both interpretations show what an important part God's truth played in Timothy's life and in his response to the false teaching. The best way to refute untruth is to know, to follow, and to proclaim the truth.

As we have seen, our response to false teaching is many faceted. First, we must know what this false teaching is. Second, we must not be afraid to condemn it. Third, we must show why it is wrong. Fourth, we must be faithful in guiding those we lead to a proper response to this false teaching. Fifth, we must make sure that we are constantly exposed to the true teaching.

PERSONAL APPLICATION

1. What false teachings and ideas do those you lead encounter? How do you plan to respond to them?

2. Write down the scheme you propose to use for studying the whole Word of God. Make sure that you expose yourself to the different parts of Scripture.

EIGHT
THE GODLINESS
OF THE LEADER (4:7, 8)

In the last chapter, we began our study of Paul's description of a good minister of Christ. We saw that the minister is one who warns those in his care about the dangers and errors of false teaching and helps them adequately to face this false teaching (4:6a). Then we saw that he is one who is constantly nourished by the Word of God, and one who practices what it teaches (4:6b). Paul also pointed out two more qualities of a good minister (v. 7).

HE REFUSES TO DABBLE IN FALSE DOCTRINES (4:7a)

The first quality has to do with the leader's relationship to false teaching. Paul said "Have nothing to do with godless myths and old wives tales" (4:7a). Earlier Paul had indicated the value of living according to the good doctrine (4:6). Now with some very strong language Paul asked Timothy to stay away from bad doctrine.

This false doctrine is described first as "godless myths." The word "godless" is accurately translated as "profane." Those who teach it may profess to be religious. But this word points to the bankruptcy of their religion. Then Paul described the false teaching as "old wives tales." William Hendriksen describes these as "silly superstitions which old women sometimes try to palm off on their neighbors or on their grandchildren."

Paul was very firm about the point he was making here and so he used some strong language. Some immature and shallow people may be attracted to this type of teaching. But Timothy was to have "nothing to do with" it. Again Paul used another severe word which suggests a strong refusal.

A good minister does not dabble in bad doctrine, however attractive it may be. If it is not found in God's Word, then he will not teach it, even if, by teaching it, he could attract a large crowd of followers.

TRAINING ONESELF IN GODLINESS (4:7b)

After the negative command to reject bad doctrine, Paul, in a manner characteristic of him, gives some positive advice: "Train yourself in godliness" (4:7b). A good minister is a godly person.

The root meaning of "godliness" conveys the idea of an attitude of reverence and awe in the presence of a majestic God. The result of such an attitude is the true worship of God, which befits that awe. Also resulting from it is active obedience to God which befits that reverence (taken from Barclay, *New Testament Words,* Westminster Press, 1974). One who lives with such an attitude of reverence resulting in worship and obedience is going to gradually become like the One he reveres. So one is called godly because he is Godlike. Others see him and say "that is what God is like." So then, to be godly is to be like God.

We must not forget that in this passage Paul was dealing with Timothy's response to false teaching. Paul had just told Timothy to combat this teaching with a careful counterteaching of orthodox truth (4:1-6). But orthodoxy without godliness is powerless in battling for the Kingdom. It dishonors the King by being unlike him and sends out inaccurate messages about the principles of the Kingdom.

I took a course in seminary in which we spent a lot of time studying the various challenges to the orthodox view of the Old Testament. In one of his lectures, almost as an aside, our teacher described how students from evangelical colleges doing post-graduate degrees in secular universities were bombarded by a low view of the Bible. There was great force in this new approach to the Bible because the lives of some of the professors who taught these views seemed to exemplify what the Bible taught about

Christian character. The bewildered students contrasted these lives with the poor examples of Christian behavior set by some of the teachers at the evangelical colleges from which they came. Not a few of these students abandoned their evangelical convictions.

Providentially, our Old Testament teacher, who upheld an orthodox view of the Bible, was both a scholar and a saint. Needless to say, I came out of that class not only convinced about the authenticity of the Old Testament but also excited about the field of Old Testament study.

So godliness was to be one of Timothy's weapons against false teaching. Because it was so important in Timothy's ministry, Paul asked him to "train" himself in godliness. The Greek verb translated "train" *(gymnazo)* is an athletic word from which we get the English "gymnasium." It means to exert oneself, to endure strenuous training.

How can one train oneself in godliness? Hendriksen gives three helpful comparisons between physical and spiritual training in his comment on this verse:

First, the athlete in the gymnasium exerts himself to the utmost. In the same way, the Christian also should, by God's power, spare no efforts to attain his goal. Is he uncertain about an area in his walk with God? unsure about how he should respond to an enemy? about whether a particular habit of his is pleasing to God? about whether the girl he is interested in is God's chosen person for him? about whether his present attitude to his job and to his possessions has conceded too much to materialism? If he has such uncertainties, he will not relax until he has discovered what God's mind is on these matters. He will ask others for advice. He will search the Scriptures and read books. He will pray about it and get others to pray. Such is the seriousness with which he approaches his training in godliness.

Second, Hendriksen says the youth discards every handicap or burden in order that he may train more freely. Similarly, the Christian divests himself of everything that could encumber his spiritual progress. Is it a relationship? a habit? his job? his ambition? His love for God and his passion for obedience is such that, even though giving up something is difficult, he will do so because of his overriding desire to be godly. If he is not sure, he is willing if necessary to deprive himself of pleasure or reward rather than risk disobeying God. He always asks God, "Is there anything in my life that may not be pleasing to you?" The moment he sees something that isn't, he battles to give it up.

The quest of many Christians today seems to be to find out how far they can go into the world without disobeying God's explicit commands. They have forgotten, as another passage about athletics suggests, that there are weights which are not specifically called sins but of which we must divest ourselves if we are to run the race well (Heb. 12:1, 2). Many today, by "flirting" with the world, are so encumbered by weights that they make no progress in their spiritual life. These people are looking for a Christianity that is both legitimate and yet has as much of the "world" as they could possibly squeeze in. As the saying goes, they want "the best of both worlds."

Such a condition has arisen, I believe, because they have continued to allow the desires of this world to have a firm foothold on their thought life. They have spent a lot of time letting society, with its warped sense of values, influence them through its books, television, and films. But the Word of God has not been allowed to have a counteracting influence on their lives. They have not lingered long enough in the Bible to let its thoughts sink into their thought life. So, unconsciously, the desires that govern much of their thinking are worldly. Their standards are the standards of the world. They look at success the way society looks at success. They look at failure the way society looks at failure.

They will, of course, stay away from the big sins. But they will cut down their catalogue of "don'ts" as much as possible. They seem to have reversed the whole process. Instead of looking for weights to divest, they are struggling to see how many uncertain areas they can keep on. Their desire to identify with the world has eclipsed their desire to identify with Christ.

What a contrast Paul was! A good example of Paul's attitude appears in 1 Corinthians 9, a chapter which concludes with one of his great athletic passages (9:25-27). At the start of this chapter he talked about his legitimate rights—rights which he could have asserted without anyone's blaming him for doing do. Then he said, "But I have not used any of these rights" (9:15). Later he said, "Though I am free and belong to no man, I make myself a slave to everyone, to win as many as possible" (9:19).

Here we see a man with a passion. He was not asking, "How

much can I enjoy and get away with?" Rather, he was saying "What I can legitimately enjoy I do away with because I am, as an athlete, a person on a special mission" (see 9:23). Clothes that are perfectly legitimate for others are not suitable for the athlete. He has a race to win. Normal clothes are too heavy for running. The athlete's eyes are fixed on that finishing tape (9:24). It is not surprising, then, to hear from such a man the words: "I beat my body and make it my slave" (9:27). So the one who trains himself to be godly divests himself of all weights that hinder him in his quest for spiritual growth.

We have already alluded to Hendriksen's third point. He says that, just as the athlete has his eyes on a goal, so we should constantly be aiming at our spiritual objective—namely that of self-dedication to God in Christ. We always keep this objective before us. We want to be like Jesus. If we are honest, we will realize that we have not attained this goal. Therefore, we will strain every spiritual muscle to attain it. Paul described this stirringly in another of his great athletic passages, Philippians 3:12-14:

Not that I have already obtained all this, or have already been made perfect, but I press on to take hold of that for which Christ Jesus took hold of me. . . . One thing I do: Forgetting what lies behind, and straining forward to what lies ahead, I press on toward the goal to win the prize for which God has called me heavenward in Christ Jesus.

Paul had a goal before him. Like an athlete today has a stopwatch with him in his practices to check up on how he is faring in relation to his goal, Paul also regularly checked up on how he was faring in relation to his goal. Spiritual inventories must have been a regular part of his life. Certainly we do know that he was straining every spiritual muscle and pressing on, refusing to relax until he reached his goal.

THE REWARDS OF GODLINESS (4:8)

Paul, continuing with the training metaphor, pointed out the value of godliness in one's personal life: "For physical training is of some value, but godliness has value for all things, holding promise for both the present life and the life to come" (v. 8).

Paul said that physical training was not intrinsically evil. We saw in our study of the doctrine of creation in chapter 7 that, because the world is God's creation and is therefore good, we need to approach the affairs of this world with the attitude that we are doing God's work. We need to work hard at the things of this world, a principle that applies not only to athletics but also to our other earthly pursuits such as our studies, our career, our business or job, our physical beauty and health, and our family responsibilities.

All these things are good, but there are many who live as if the things of this world are most important. Such people may at times be willing to sacrifice spiritual growth in order to advance in these things. Paul was asking them to seek a proper balance. We often hear people say that, because they are so busy, they have no time for such things as prayer and Bible study, Christian service, or worship on the Lord's Day. They have lost their sense of proportion. They are pursuing things of limited value and neglecting the most important thing—the task of cultivating their relationship with God.

Note how Paul described the value of godliness. He said it "has value for all things, holding promise for both the present life and the world to come." It has "value for all things." Godliness helps not only in so-called religious matters but in every area of life. Its value is not only for the world to come but also for the present life.

Earlier we said that some give up godliness because they want to have the best of both worlds. But they don't. Instead, they have very little in this world and nothing in the next. It is the Christian who has the best of both worlds. God created this world and so only those who follow him can have the best of this world.

At first, it may not be apparent that godliness holds promise for the present life. Indeed, sin is rampant today and Satan has so much power that Paul calls him "the god of this world" (2 Cor. 4:4). It looks as if the godly miss out on the best of life, that they are put down and cannot succeed in society because of their principles. But they alone know life in all its fullness (John 10:10), because the One whom they serve is the One who created life. Notice just one aspect of this full life we enjoy on earth—the quality of peace. The word "peace" means many things in the Bible. But when used of God's gift to man it basically means general well-being or wholeness. A person with peace is in harmony with God, with himself, and with the world around him. He knows God is sovereign over all the circumstances of life. Therefore, he views life positively. To put it another way, he is truly happy to be alive. He knows his future is secure. He does not suffer from guilt over the past because his sins have been washed by the blood of Christ. He is at peace. No wonder John Wesley said, "Oh what a pearl, of great price, is the lowest degree of the peace of God." It is worth selling everything in order to receive.

Such peace the godless do not have. They have sought security from the things of this world. But this world is full of uncertainty. As Jesus put it, "Moth and rust destroy and . . . thieves break in and steal" (Matt. 6:19). In today's language, this could be expanded thus: Markets fluctuate and sales are lost; economic conditions change and money loses its value, political policies change and thriving businesses or lands or houses are nationalized, climatic conditions change and crops are lost. To pursue the things of the world is to pursue uncertainty. Therefore if you put your trust in things of the world, you will lose your peace.

But God does not change. Through every experience, we have the assurance: "The Lord will fulfill his purpose for me" (Ps. 138:8). So we have peace. We have the assurance that because the Lord is our shepherd we will not be in need of anything (Ps. 23:1).

How sad it is to see so many people who have worked hard to succeed in life, but who have neglected the things of God! At the end of their lives they are disillusioned because success did not produce the desired effect. Godliness is the only thing that can give us the best of this world.

Godliness, Paul said, gives us the best of the world to come also. Three qualities of that coming world will explain why this is true. First, in the world to come secrets are revealed (Luke 12:2, 3). Today we do certain things and think no one knows. We bribe, we lie, we pretend, we lust, we maneuver, we push ourselves forward, and we say, "No one will find out about how we did it." But in the next world our deeds will be made known. And for many it will be a time of shame.

The sinful deeds of the godly, on the other hand, have been confessed. Therefore they are erased and forgotten. The godly have no exposure to fear as their slate is clean. The only things to be exposed are what is recorded in the Book of Life and these are their good deeds (Rev. 20:11-15).

The second quality of the world to come is that in that world the

principle of retribution will operate. Today it seems to be inopera-
tive, since many people get away with evil. They find that evil
works. They think that honesty does not pay. But they are very
shortsighted, for in the next world, when the principle of retribution will be operative, some will receive the reward they await, but
others will receive the punishment due.

The loss we suffer in this world for the sake of godliness is
nothing in comparison to the reward that awaits us. The prospect
of that reward lightens the present suffering. So Paul could say,
"Our light and momentary troubles are achieving for us an eternal
glory that far outweighs them all" (2 Cor. 4:17). In reality these
troubles of Paul were extremely severe, as the context shows
(2 Cor. 4:8-12). But in comparison to the glory, they were insignificant.

On the other hand, Jesus called an extremely successful farmer
a fool because he had achieved all that the world could give, but he
was not rich toward God (Luke 12:20, 21). When he died, all he
had was the punishment he was to face.

The third quality of the world to come is that joy or regret will
then be made perfect. For some there is going to be the joy of
participating in Christ's total victory. There is going to be the joy
of perfecting a love relationship. There is going to be the joy of
completing our destiny, when we become exactly what we should
be and are presently striving to be. Today we groan and travail,
waiting for our adoption as sons, the redemption of our bodies
(Rom. 8:20-23). On that day all these things which we presently
know and experience in part will be perfected. Accompanying this
perfection of our destiny is the perfection of joy.

But for others it is the perfection of regret. Punishment is
complete. The reality of the wrong choices they made is also
completely visible. Naturally they experience the totality of regret.

With such facts before him, it is not surprising that Paul's mind
was filled with thoughts of heaven. So intense was his love for
heaven that at one time he confessed that he wished he could go
there right away (Phil. 1:23). Of course, God wanted him to stay
on. But while he remained on earth his mind was set on things
above (Col. 3:1).

Paul sought to give Timothy this perspective of eternity in these
letters. So, in addition to the text we are presently studying, there
are other passages which speak of the world to come. Paul asked
Timothy to teach the rich to lay up treasures for the world to

come by being generous and willing to share of their wealth
(1 Tim. 6:18, 19). When charging him about being faithful in
performing his ministry, Paul reminded him of the judgment he
was to face one day which is given as an incentive to faithfulness in
ministry (2 Tim. 4:1, 2). This verse is reminiscent of 2 Corinthians
5:10 and 11 where, after talking about how we must all stand
before the judgment seat, Paul said, "Therefore knowing the fear
of the Lord, we persuade men." The prospect of judgment
motivated him to ministry.

Second Timothy 4:6-8 is the classic autobiographical statement
of Paul's perspective of eternity:

*For I am already being poured out like a drink offering, and the time
has come for my departure. I have fought the good fight, I have
finished the race, I have kept the faith. Now there is in store for me
the crown of righteousness, which the Lord, the righteous Judge, will
award to me on that day—and not only to me, but also to all who
have longed for his appearing.*

Again, just before he closed the epistle, Paul said, "The Lord
will rescue me from every evil attack and will bring me safely to
his heavenly kingdom" (2 Tim. 4:18).

This was not only an emphasis of Paul's. It is seen right through
the New Testament. How important it is then to give young
Christians a perspective of eternity. It motivates them to take the
cross and follow Jesus all the way. It helps them realize that the
price of godliness is worth paying.

Godliness is an important issue with which many sincere
Christians struggle. They ask, is it really worthwhile following
Christ's principles totally? Is the price of total dedication to Christ
worth paying? Paul would answer this with a resounding "Yes! It is
the only way for a Christian to live!"

PERSONAL APPLICATION

An athlete gives special attention in his training to areas of weakness in his life. In the same way we need to concentrate on
overcoming our weak areas. What areas of your life need special
attention? How can you adjust your "training schedule" so as to
concentrate on these areas?

NINE
A MODEL LIFE (4:9–12)

In the past two chapters we saw Paul instructing Timothy on how to deal with the false teaching he was encountering. Timothy was to expose the false teachings and show where they had gone wrong (4:1-6). Then he was to avoid having anything to do with these teachings (4:7a). And then, most importantly, he was to live a godly life (4:7b, 8). In this chapter and the next we will study more about the godly life-style of a leader, especially as it affects his example before God's people.

RESPONDING TO AN OBJECTION (4:9, 10)

Paul had said that godliness holds "promise for both the present life and the life to come" (v. 8). With such a prospect of reward for godliness before him, Paul said, "We labor and strive" (4:10).

Paul's opponents would have said to this, "Don't be so sure of these eternal rewards." For, according to their teaching, only the spiritual elite, those who have had special experiences and who had received special knowledge, could be sure of full and final salvation.

Against such teaching Paul affirmed: "This is a trustworthy saying that deserves full acceptance. . . . that we have put our hope in the living God, who is the Savior of all men, and especially of those who believe" (4:9, 10). Paul was saying here that we can be sure of final triumph. There is no need for uncertainty about this, because God, in whom we have placed our trust, is the

Savior of all men. All kinds of people, rich and poor, educated and uneducated, Jew and Gentile, can be assured of the fullness of God's final salvation. If we strive for godliness, placing our hope in him whatever our background may be, God will grant us salvation.

This verse does not say that every person who ever lived is going to be saved, as some have supposed. It was for this reason that Paul added "and especially of those who believe." Christ's salvation is available for all to accept, but only those who believe appropriate it. While God is potentially the Savior of all, he is in fact the Savior of only the believers.

SILENCING CRITICISM THROUGH EXAMPLE (4:12)

Paul gave a charge to Timothy to be faithful in the teaching ministry (v. 11). Then Paul went on to focus on Timothy's personal life as it related to his need to be a good example (4:12-16).

Paul first said, "Don't let anyone look down on you because you are young." Timothy had obviously been encountering some resistance to his leadership because of his age. The word translated "young" was used in the first century for people up to the age of forty. Many scholars place Timothy's age when the Epistles were written around the mid-thirties. At that age he would still be considered relatively young.

Yet, Timothy was the head of a large church, supervising leaders who were older than he, people who had previously been supervised by the great Apostle Paul himself. Some of these leaders would not have been too enthusiastic about being led by a youngster. The false teachers may also have used his age as a weapon to undermine his authority.

The problem of not being respected is one that many young Christians face. It is overcome not by exerting oneself in an authoritarian manner. Such a reaction would only add fuel to the fire of criticism against him and would be used as yet another example of his immaturity and incompetence.

Nor can the problem of not being respected be overcome by insisting on conformity to some rules or by appealing to the policies of the church or organization. Indeed, rules must be enforced, but trying to enforce them at such a time is an inadequate means to winning confidence when one's leadership abilities are already being questioned. Besides, in the Kingdom of

God life is not governed by the letter of the law but by the freedom of the Spirit.

Neither can a leader under the pressure of criticism give up the asserting of the authority rightfully his as leader of the group. Some are prone to give in when their authority is questioned and let a kind of democratic system rule. What the majority wants is what is done. Committees or a few influential people run the show. But when this happens, there is no clear sense of leadership in the group. Such a situation is alien to the biblical picture of God's community, as a people under the clear leadership of leaders who represent God. A leader is one who has been appointed to lead the people and he cannot abdicate this responsibility when the going gets tough.

Elsewhere Paul warned Timothy that he must not give in to his natural tendency to timidity because, over and above his natural weaknesses, God had endowed him with a spirit of power, of love and of self-discipline (2 Tim. 1:7).

What then is the solution for a leader under fire? Paul said the solution was an exemplary life: "Set an example for the believers in speech, in life, in love, in faith and in purity." The way to silence criticism and to win confidence is by earning respect through an exemplary life.

Timothy's reputation was at stake. The way to overcome the problem was not by a powerful public relations drive, which leaders today are prone to try, but by an exemplary life. When we take care of our character, our reputation takes care of itself.

The Greek word translated "example" is the word *tupos* from which we get the word "type." The Christian leader, then, is a type or model whom others could follow.

Paul went on to mention two areas where Timothy's example needed to be evident. He first mentioned "speech," referring to Paul's day to day conversation rather than his ministry of preaching, which is brought up in the next verse.

The Bible, especially Proverbs and James, has a lot to say about the power of the tongue as an agent for good and for evil. Speech is particularly important for leaders not only because leaders are a type for others to follow but also because what they say affects a wide spectrum of people. What a leader says is taken seriously because it comes from the head and thus represents the group which he leads.

There is too much at stake in the leader's example for him to neglect spiritual speech defects. He must always ask himself, Does what I say judge sin? Does it uphold righteousness? Does it communicate love? Does it edify? Does it draw people to Christ? and most of all, Does it honor Christ? The constant prayer of the sincere leader is "Set a guard over my mouth, O Lord; keep watch over the door of my lips" (Ps. 141:3).

The next area in which Timothy's example was to be seen was what Paul called his "life," referring to his behavior or style of life. Paul was saying, let the way you behave, the way you go about your daily business, be such that people who were intending to criticize you would end up being challenged by your example.

After giving two areas where Timothy's example should be evident, Paul moves to enumerate three qualities which that example should contain.

He started with "love," that greatest of words in the Christian vocabulary. Love is the greatest determining factor in all Christian behavior, which is why the Christian makes love his aim (1 Cor. 14:1).

When Paul wrote this letter, Timothy was under pressure from his opponents. He would be tempted to retaliate, to "teach them a lesson," to make a cutting remark that would put them in their places. Yet the battles of the Kingdom are not won by the methods of Satan. So, no matter what other people would do to him or say about him, he was to seek only their good. He was never to be bitter, never resentful, never vengeful; he was never to allow himself to hate; he was never to refuse to forgive.

It has never been easy to practice this principle of Christian love. Unloving responses to various situations seem to be able to produce quick results. But one day we will realize that the most effective and the only appropriate path to take in any situation is the path of love, that the way of love never fails (1 Cor. 13:8). A beautiful example of the power of love in the midst of opposition comes from the life of Sadhu Sundar Singh. Let Mrs. Rebecca Parker tell the story.

One morning a number of Sadhus were gathered on the banks of the Ganges at a place called Rishi Kesh amidst a crowd of religious bathers, and amongst them stood Sadhu Sundar Singh, Testament in hand, preaching. Some were listening in a mildly interested way, whilst others joked and scoffed at the man and his message. Unexpectedly a man from the crowd lifted up a handful of sand and threw it in his eyes, an act that roused the indignation of a better-disposed man, who handed the offender over to a policeman. Meanwhile the Sadhu went down to the river and washed the sand from his eyes. Upon his return he begged for the release of the culprit and proceeded with his preaching. Surprised by this act and the way he had taken the insult, the man, Vidyananda, fell at his feet begging his forgiveness, and declaring a desire to understand more about what the Sadhu was speaking about. This man became a seeker after truth, and afterwards accompanied him on his journey, learning with meekness from his lips the story of redeeming love (Sadhu Sundar Singh, *Madras: The Christian Literature Society, 1918).*

Within every man and woman, even within those who oppose the godly, is a desire for God and his ways, a built-in thirst (Acts 17:27) that many people may not acknowledge. Many believe that they cannot live the life of righteousness and love even though that is the ideal. They feel it is impractical in this society in which evil has taken such a firm hold, so they reject this way. But they cannot destroy the thirst.

When such a person sees in another the qualities which he wishes he himself had, he becomes receptive. A message of hope is sent to him saying, "So, it is not impractical after all. Here is a man who has tried this way and for him it seems to work." Some disregard this message. Others pay attention to it and inquire further and the door is opened to present the gospel. How powerful a force for good, in a world that has become cynical about sincerity and religion, is true Christian love enfleshed in a real person.

The next quality Paul mentioned was "faith." Our trust in God is constantly put to the test as we encounter problems of various sorts. Under such conditions we may be tempted to adopt an unchristian response because it promises to bring a quick solution to the problem. Or we may give in to despair. Or we may react irrationally, without self-control due to the pressure placed upon us. These reactions stem from a lack of faith in God and his promises.

It is amidst crisis that a leader's faith is put to the test. His faith will help him to persevere in God's way, confident that God will act on his behalf. So he will not compromise or despair or give up. Such leaders will help the fainthearted to continue to trust in God amidst crises and thus help them to persevere along the path of obedience.

What if the leader's faith fails and he acts in a way that reflects this failure? He could communicate to those under him the message that the Christian gospel does not have within it the resources to face crises triumphantly. His poor example could contribute to the people of God living in defeat amidst crisis.

In Acts 4 we see how the faith of the leaders of the early church helped them come out of their first major crisis triumphantly. In this chapter is the record of the first instance of active official opposition to the cause of the gospel that the early church experienced. Peter and John were "commanded . . . not to speak or teach at all in the name of Jesus" (4:18). Then they were threatened further and let go (4:21). They went back to the church and reported what happened (4:23). The church immediately began to pray. But the content of their prayer was surprising. They started by addressing God as "Sovereign Lord" (4:24).

Then they described in some detail how this sovereignty of God was manifested in creation (4:24) and in the course of history (4:25-28). Only at the end of their prayer was their problem mentioned, and that too in passing as a prelude to their request for the ability to "speak (God's) Word with great boldness" (4:29).

God answered that prayer for boldness. But their troubles intensified, climaxing in the death of Stephen and the ensuing persecution resulting in the scattering of the church.

At first this persecution and scattering would have looked like tragedy. But looking back, Luke would have seen the marvelous providence of God. So when describing the "scattering," he did not use the usual word (Acts 8:1, 4). He used instead the word *diaspeiro,* which means "to scatter as seed is scattered on the ground." Looking back at this scattering, the church regarded it as providential, for it enabled the church to fulfill Christ's great commission to preach the gospel to all the world. So Luke said, "Those who had been scattered preached the word wherever they went" (Acts 8:4). As one writer puts it, "The people went as missionaries more than as refugees" (Everett Harrison, *Acts: The Expanding Church,* Moody Press, 1975). God had indeed worked out his sovereign will. The faith reflected in that prayer of Acts 4 was not unfounded. And the request for boldness resulting from the belief in sovereignty was the only appropriate response to the crisis. It shows us how faith helps a whole people to persevere amidst crisis.

The third quality which Timothy's example should reflect was "purity," referring likely to two areas. The first area we could call moral purity. It refers to such things as chastity in matters of sex. We know of the need there is today for leaders who are an example in this area. Society is bombarding us with moral impurity. The media, the novels, the ordinary conversations of people, the jokes people tell—all seem to thrust on us the idea that sex being exclusively for marriage is an outmoded and unexciting belief. People are accepting, in varying degrees, the idea that they could have sexual enjoyment outside of marriage. We see it in books, films, jokes, in what passes off as innocent touching and physical contact with members of the opposite sex and, in its extreme, in sexual relationships outside of marriage.

Christians growing up in such a society struggle to remain pure, especially because they themselves struggle with the sinful nature that delights in the illegitimate use of human desires. With such a background, what a need there is for Christian leaders who, by their pure lives and teaching, will pave the way for a bewildered generation to live pure lives! What a need for leaders whom to be with is an encouragement to purity and a rebuke to impurity, whose lives are vibrant examples of the beauty and joy of holy living!

The second area of "purity" concerns integrity of heart. The idea is that of acting out of pure motives. In such a cynical age as ours, there have been so many insincere people in positions of leadership that many people find it hard to believe that leaders could act out of pure motives.

This cynicism has invaded the church too. Discerning people find it difficult to believe that leaders serve only because of love for God and man. They see workers upset when others reap the harvest where they have done the sowing. They hear one leader speak ill of another. They listen to a leader make use of every opportunity to boast about his achievements. They see rivalry. They read reports of work which are not quite accurate. They observe the complex maneuverings of ecclesiastical politics. They see leaders hurt and angry when they are not given due recognition. And gradually the message sinks in: These people are in it for personal gain and glory.

What a breath of fresh air a leader with sincere motives would be in such an environment, someone whose only motives in life are the glory of God and the service of man! One whose behavior does not betray ulterior motives! Such a leader would help people believe once again that it is possible for people to be sincere, that it is indeed possible to serve God out of honest motives. Here then is a goal to set before us—to be examples in love, faith and purity.

WHAT IF WE FAIL?

We all know, however, that none of us as leaders conforms totally to this biblical standard. How should we respond to our imperfection? Certainly not by excusing it.

There is a dangerous tendency among Christians to consider sin as inevitable and thus excusable. So we find bumper stickers like, "Christians are not perfect, just forgiven," proclaiming to the world that shortcomings should be excused. Nothing short of total obedience is normal for one who follows a resurrected and victorious Master.

Indeed the shortcomings of a leader could have dangerous consequences within the Christian community. Some could use his shortcomings as an excuse for their own sinfulness. Some could use them to discredit his leadership. Worst of all, God is dishonored because his representative has failed.

The only solution is for him to accept his failure, and to repent of his sin. If the believers have been affected then he will have to face up to it squarely in front of them.

A quick apology, which could be just a way to avoid responsibility for his actions, will not solve the problem. Some leaders think that simply by saying, "I'm sorry if I did anything wrong," they will undo all the damage that has been done. Christian confession is very different than this. The word for confession in the New Testament (*homologeo*) means "to say the same thing as." To confess is to come to terms fully with the issue and to say the same thing as God, who knows the truth, says about it.

Instead of saying "sorry," he may have to say, "I made a very unkind statement. I hurt you by it. I have no excuse to give. Please forgive me and be assured that I will do everything in my power to erase the ill effects of that statement. I will write to Bill and tell him that what I said was wrong."

This radical type of response will be very humbling for a leader. But even though he is humbled, God is glorified. And the glory of God is the leader's primary concern. In fact, because the leader is united with God, he shares the glory. He rejoices that God's name has been cleared, that the ill effects of his bad example have been erased, that the door has been opened once again for effective ministry.

PERSONAL APPLICATION

Recall the last time you came under heavy criticism. How did you respond to this criticism? In the light of what you learned from this lesson, should you have responded differently?

TEN
A MODEL MINISTRY (4:13–16b)

Paul told Timothy how to silence criticism by leading a model life (4:12). Next he showed him how to have a model ministry. Paul told Timothy that he must not only lead an exemplary life, but he must also be an excellent minister (4:13-15). Throughout this study we will see this dual emphasis.

Sometimes we hear people say, "He's a great saint, but he does not prepare his sermons too well." Other times we hear people say, "He's a great preacher, but he has a terrible temper." You cannot divorce life from ministry. And anyone who does not diligently pursue both areas is a failure by God's standards.

Paul in this section described six features of a model ministry.

DEVOTION TO PUBLIC MINISTRY (4:13)

Paul first said that Timothy was to "devote [himself] to the public reading of Scripture, to preaching and to teaching" (4:13). Here are three vital aspects of public ministry, all relating to the Word of God. We are familiar with preaching and teaching, which involve proclaiming what the Word says. But "the public reading of Scripture" has not been given much emphasis today. Its importance has been grossly underrated in evangelical circles. It is often so poorly done that many Christians regard it as the least meaningful segment of a worship service.

The word translated "devote" here *(prosecho)*, literally meaning "give heed or attendance to," implies preparation in advance. This gives us our first key to effective ministry. Because the model minister devotes himself to his public ministry, he prepares himself adequately before he goes before the people with his message.

Realizing how important it is he gives it due priority in his ministry. There has been a reaction against public ministry in many Christian circles today. Personal ministry, small group ministry, counseling ministry and ministries using such media as television, film, music, and drama have grown greatly in importance lately. With this, the traditional preaching and teaching ministries seem to have diminished in importance.

Indeed, preaching is a greater challenge now than it was a few generations ago. John Stott, in his book, *I Believe in Preaching,* (London: Hodder & Stoughton, 1982), has discussed three main features in modern Western society which make public ministry a particularly challenging task. What he says of the West applies in many areas of the East too. These features are the anti-authority mood of today, the cybernetics revolution (radical changes in communication as a result of the development of complex electronic equipment), and the churches' loss of confidence in the gospel.

Those of us who work among non-Western non-Christians are also given the enormous challenge of getting people to understand our message. Eastern politeness opens many to listen to us. But often they don't understand what we are saying. Our categories of thought take so much of Christian background for granted that those without a Christian background find it difficult to figure out what we are trying to say. So whether we come from the East or from the West, if we are committed to public ministry, we have a big challenge ahead of us.

The challenge may be to win a hearing among those who are not used to listening or not interested in listening, or it may be to make our message understood by those who think very differently than us. This challenges us to devote ourselves afresh to public ministry. We must sharpen our skills of communication, which comes only through hard work. For those seeking to dig deeper into this I recommend Stott's book, *I Believe in Preaching.* For those working with non-Christians the best book I know for the nonspecialist is John T. Seamands' book, *Tell It Well: Communicating the Gospel Across Cultures* (Beacon Hill Press, 1981).

BEING CAREFUL ABOUT OUR GIFT (4:14)

After listing the public ministries Timothy was to have, Paul told him, "Do not neglect your gift, which was given you through a prophetic message when the body of elders laid their hands on you" (4:14). At some special event the elders had laid hands on Timothy. It may have been at his ordination as leader of the Ephesian church, before Paul's departure from there, but we cannot be sure of this. When this took place, a prophetic message had been received through which Timothy's particular ministry gift was confirmed to him. What that gift was we do not know.

This passage, however, does tell us something of the role others play in the discovery of one's spiritual gifts. With the formation of a definite body or canon of Scripture, prophecies as direct words from God to particular situations became less important in the church. We cannot say they were lost completely. But certainly most of us today do not discover our gifts through prophetic utterances.

Yet other people still play an important part in helping Christians discover their gifts. They observe a person and receive God-directed prophetic insight about his potential and communicate this insight to him. Through this that person can discover his particular gift. The Bible teaches we all receive particular gifts from God (1 Cor. 12). One of our great responsibilities is to find out what those gifts are and to use them diligently.

This verse suggests that the gift could be neglected. The word Paul used literally means "to be careless about something." Gifted preachers can end up ineffective after a few years of ministry if they don't study diligently the Word and prepare their sermons. It is possible to allow other activities to fill our schedule so much that we cannot find the time to concentrate on our gifts.

One of the saddest sights in the church today is that of a person, richly gifted in preaching, teaching, or counseling, who is unable to give much time to his particular gift because he has "risen" (!) to the top of his organization or church, so that he has no time for these ministries. He has too many meetings to attend, too many administrative duties to fulfill. He may speak in numerous places, but as you listen to him you realize that he has gone stale. He has not been giving enough time for fresh thinking, for hard preparation. He needs to reorder his priorities even if it means a drop in status or salary.

This verse shows that our gifts have a divine and a human side to them. It is God who sovereignly gives them to us as he wills. He may even use others to communicate to us what the gift is. But it is our duty to carefully cultivate the gift.

DILIGENCE IN MINISTRY (4:15a)

The third statement Paul made about the model ministry in this passage was "Be diligent in these matters" (4:15a). The word translated "diligent" *(meletao)* is related to the word "neglect" or "careless" *(ameleo)* in verse 14. It can mean "to study, to prosecute diligently." It carries the idea of taking pains over our ministry.

Lethargy could set in in our lives, so we must take heed lest we be satisfied with a job not well done. Whatever we do must be done to the best of our ability, whether it is reading a lesson, or singing, or preaching, or teaching, or visiting, or typing, or getting a handbill ready, or discipling, or counseling. Sometimes when we hear a sermon we can discern without much effort that the preacher is not well prepared. He may be rambling, or his sermon may lack solid content. That preacher has been lazy. He has not been diligent in his preparation.

Laziness is a common problem in the Christian ministry and full-time workers are particularly susceptible to it. As W. E. Sangster puts it, lay people who are lazy have to keep certain hours at their work place, otherwise they will be dismissed. Ministers on the other hand "are largely masters of their own time. . . . No clock records the minister's hour of beginning and no machine can measure the earnestness with which he goes at his work once he has begun." Sangster goes on to say, "If a man's conscience concerning time gets dulled through the years, it is amazing how busy he can feel while he is doing very little" *(The Approach to Preaching,* Baker, 1974).

Sangster sees the answer to this peril "in a disciplined devotional life." I must say that this is not the answer I expected from Sangster. But what he says makes sense: "A man who goes over his day each evening with God will not long remain satisfied with pottering, sluggishness, and days half frittered away." Sangster here is bringing up one of his favorite themes—the need to develop a system of checks through which we can see how we are faring in our walk with God. He has in fact written a book entitled, *A Spiritual Check-up* (London: Epworth Press, 1966), a book consisting of scores of questions the Christian asks himself about his own life.

In the same way, the Christian worker always asks whether he has been diligent in what he has done. For example, at the end of a meeting he asks, "How did I preach today? Was I properly prepared?" Or he may ask at the end of the day, "Did I make the most of my time today? Was there anything I did that was a waste of time?" With such an attitude a person can ensure that his ministry will be characterized by that excellence which honors the name of Christ.

ABSORPTION IN MINISTRY (4:15b)

Paul then told Timothy: "Give yourself wholly to them [matters concerning his ministry]" (4:15b). This brings us to the fourth important feature about Christian ministry. We are dealing here with two words, which literally translate as "be in." The idea is that of being absorbed in the work we do. Our lives are wrapped up in our ministry. We don't do our ministry half-heartedly like fulfilling a necessary duty.

Sometimes we hear preachers who utter their truths in a mechanical manner. Their content may be good. They may have diligently done their preparation. But their delivery lacks fire. They put their listeners into a mental stupor. They are unable to motivate them to arise from their spiritual slumber and follow Christ wholly. They need to become absorbed, to become gripped by the truth of the gospel.

The people whom God uses mightily are people with a passion. In a time of great crisis and humiliation, when Jeremiah was tempted to give up preaching, he confessed, "His word is in my heart like a burning fire, shut up in my bones. I am weary of holding it in; indeed, I cannot" (Jer. 20:9). He was not weary of preaching. He was weary of not preaching! Paul said, "I cannot boast, for I am compelled to preach. Woe to me if I do not preach the gospel" (1 Cor. 9:16). Benjamin Franklin said he often went to hear George Whitefield because there, before his eyes, he could watch a man burn (from Donald E. Demaray's *Preacher Aflame*, Baker, 1972).

This fire must not be confused with the vibrancy and bounciness which is only a personality trait of a few people. Even people without a fiery personality could become fiery in ministry as the truth of God's Word grips them and the Holy Spirit burns into their hearts its reality. They burn with a desire to have the fire of love overflow from their lives into their ministries. Charles Simeon, a British evangelical minister in the Anglican church who had a wide and lasting ministry, is a good example of a man who was not by nature vibrant but became so in ministry. F. W. Boreham has this to say about him:

His style of speech is not prepossessing. His voice is weak and unmusical; his address is by no means graceful; and, viewed from some angles his appearance is a little grotesque. But, as soon as he becomes impassioned, we forget all about that. His voice becomes fervent and compelling, his gestures, becoming more natural as he becomes less nervous, are expressive of an intense desire to convey the full force of his argument or appeal; he strikes you as feeling deeply over every word that he utters; his face is illumined by intensity and pleasant animation. (Daily Readings from F. W. Boreham, London: Hodder & Stoughton, 1976.)

W. E. Sangster in one of his great books on preaching, *Power in Preaching* (Baker, 1976), has a chapter entitled "Glow over It." He starts the chapter with these words:

Some preaching fails in power because it fails in passion. It may be intellectually respectable, the points the sermon sets out to make may be well made and worth making, but there is no glow about it. The people depart, but they are inwardly unmoved, and they are unmoved because the preacher himself was unmoved" (p. 86).

Sangster gives four ways passion can come into our preaching and this advice applies to all other aspects of ministry. He says, "Prayer is the chief way." He describes a powerful black preacher who said that in his preparation for the pulpit he "read himself full" and "thought himself clear" and also "prayed himself hot." All our involvement in Christian work must be bathed in prayer. Prayer helps us maintain a warm relationship with God, and passion emerges from that relationship.

Then, Sangster says, the preacher must believe in the power of preaching. He must have faith in what he is doing. He must know that it has the power to effect something that counts for eternity.

Third, he must maintain his wonder over the gospel and the truths of God. He must not lose the freshness in his attitude toward Christianity. Sangster points out that "familiarity is one of the occupational diseases of the ministry." When we "grow familiar of awe and rapture" we lose our sense of wonder about the things of God. It is not easy to maintain a sense of wonder in this cynical age. The key to maintaining this is in our personal lives for, as Sangster puts it, "Whatever keeps wonder in a preacher's personal religion will keep wonder in his pulpit." The moment we sense that we have lost that sense of rapture over the gospel we must take remedial steps to come back to a warm relationship with the glorious truths of the gospel.

Sangster's fourth means in the path to passion is that of allowing the Holy Spirit to breathe upon us. In another book Sangster calls this "Unction" or "the plus of the Spirit" (The Approach to Preaching, Baker, 1951). What he is talking about is a state where the fresh wind of the Spirit is blowing where he wills and the preacher has hoisted his sails in such a way that his boat moves forward in the direction of the wind.

Oh, that our ministry would be moving forward with the wind of God's Spirit! It is such a thrill to sail along in his power and the excitement in our experience will be evident to those to whom we minister. They will see fire and catch it. Hearts will be ignited to share the joy and excitement that we share.

PROGRESS IN MINISTRY (4:15c)

The fifth feature about ministry in this passage is a result of diligence and absorption. Paul said, "Be diligent in these matters; give yourself wholly to them, so that everyone may see your progress." Warren Wiersbe says that this word "progress" has the idea of "pioneer advance into new territory" (Listening to the Giants, Baker, 1980). One who is progressing in ministry continues to sharpen his skills, to increase his knowledge, to deepen his dedication, and to widen his vision. So people seeing him after some time notice how much he has grown.

How does diligence and absorption in ministry facilitate progress? People who approach ministry with the attitude of diligence and absorption have such a deep desire to do their best for God that they are always aware of their shortcomings. They are not guilty of complacency and self-satisfaction. Their standards are so high that they are constantly restless, constantly aware of their need. Such restlessness is the ideal background for growth.

Needy people are always asking others to evaluate their performance, to advise them on how to do better. They are always looking for ways to renew their mind, to improve their methods, to gain more knowledge of God and of the world because they realize how much more they need to know.

Progress then is a by-product of such diligence. The diligent minister may not realize it because he is constantly aware of his inadequacies and is battling to improve. But, as Paul said, everyone else will see his progress.

We are not talking here about perfectionism, where a person drives himself to achieve, never happy with himself or his performance. Perfectionism comes out of an inner inadequacy that drives a person. Progress comes from a desire to please God. The inadequacies which cause perfectionism can be overcome when the Holy Spirit comes in and heals our hurts. The need that produces progress in ministry can coexist with peace and joy and inner satisfaction. The Christian can be satisfied in Christ and so be a well-rounded, fulfilled person. But at the same time, he can strive for a deeper life and a more effective ministry. Maturity comes when he is able to let peace and joy coexist with a sense of need and dissatisfaction.

WATCHFUL PERSEVERANCE (4:16)

Paul began by saying, "Watch your life and doctrine closely. Persevere in them" (v. 16). Paul had just said that others would see Timothy's progress. But if others were to see this, Timothy must watch his life and doctrine closely. "Watch . . . closely" is the translation of a single word *(epecho)* which means to "keep a strict eye on" something. Others see progress taking place, and it may seem to be an effortless thing. But in actual reality, progress is the result of a life of strict self-examination.

Those making pioneer advances into new territory need to give particular attention to watching their life and doctrine. As they reach out to new areas, they could discard or overlook some of the foundational aspects of Christian faith and practice. For example, an evangelical who becomes alert to social concerns could begin to neglect evangelism—a thing that has happened all too often.

Progress is adding something new to a foundation. The only foundations which are destroyed are those that do not accord with Scripture. And indeed some beliefs and practices people consider to be foundations of Christianity are not found in the Scriptures. But scriptural foundations must be clung to.

Paul described how one can watch his life and doctrine in his next statement: "Persevere in them." This meant that Timothy was to persist in the things he was taught as being basic to his belief and practice.

Consider how the watching and persevering apply to a Christian's life and doctrine. His life would include his spiritual life, his ministry life, his intellectual life, his emotional life, his family life, his physical life, and his social life. One of the greatest challenges a leader faces is that of keeping a strict eye on so many areas. He needs to be constantly checking up on how he is faring in each of them.

He may need to ask, "Is my devotional life deeper than it was a year ago?" If not, he needs to ask why and take some remedial action. He may, for example, have to drop some ministry or public activity such as membership on a committee or board so as to find more time for his family or for his personal devotions.

He may need to ask, "Am I growing as a communicator of the gospel?" or "Am I doing enough reading?" or "Am I getting enough exercise?" or "Am I having a balanced diet?" or "Am I applying my Christian principles in my job?" If his answer is "No" to any of these questions, then he must go about remedying the situation. I cannot overemphasize the need for regular spiritual inventories in the life of a Christian.

Doctrine in this verse would refer to what one believes and teaches. We could stray in doctrine, too. As we are challenged by contemporary biblical scholarship, we may veer away from a belief in the complete trustworthiness of God's Word. Contemporary culture may pressure us into accepting unbiblical attitudes to issues such as materialism, relationships with the opposite sex, lust, homosexuality, and divorce. Living in a pluralistic society, which emphasizes the importance of religious tolerance, we may become embarrassed by the biblical insistence on the uniqueness of Christianity. Such biblical teachings have rarely been popular with unbiblical people.

Many around us may defect to something less than biblical views, but we must persevere. We must not be ashamed of being branded as old-fashioned, or prudish, or antisocial, or foolish, or naive, or proud.

Persevering in faithfulness to scriptural truth must not be confused with narrow conservatism. The Bible is an active, living book that has always had a revolutionary message to every age. It has always cut at the heart of the human malady of selfishness and its various manifestations and upheld a radical holiness and love which is revolutionary in every age. Surely biblical Christianity, with its insistence on equality and a concern for the rights for the poor and the oppressed, has a radical message for our society with all its glaring inequalities.

The living nature of the Word of God necessitates that the language, the music, and the methods with which we express the gospel will change with every age, though the message remains unchanged. Some conservatives resist such changes. But biblical orthodoxy demands such changes because the unchanging gospel cries out to be heard by all peoples of all ages. The old Youth For Christ motto puts it well: "Geared to the times, and anchored to the rock."

Here then are six features of a model ministry:

1. A model minister devotes himself to public ministry.
2. He is not careless about the use of his gift.
3. He is diligent in his approach to ministry.
4. The ministry has absorbed his whole being.
5. He is constantly progressing upwards to greater effectiveness and Christlikeness.
6. He is careful to persevere in keeping his way of life and beliefs faithful to God's norms.

Paul ended this chapter by telling Timothy, "If you do [persevere with a model life and ministry], you will save both yourself and your hearers" (4:16c). That is how important an exemplary life is. Its consequences are eternal. So we feel we are justified in saying so much about it in a book on leadership.

THE PUBLIC READING OF SCRIPTURE

The public reading of Scripture is a practice which the Christians inherited from the Jewish synagogue. When Jesus went to the synagogue in Nazareth, he read from "the scroll of the prophet Isaiah" (Luke 4:16-21). An interesting description of worship in the early church comes from a defense of Christianity written by Justin Martyr around A.D. 170.

On the day called the day of the Sun a gathering takes place of all who live in the towns or in the country in one place. The memoirs of the Apostles or the writings of the prophets are read as long as time permits. Then the reader stops and the leader by word of mouth impresses and urges to the imitation of these good things. Then we all stand together and send forth prayers (First Apology, *1:67).*

In Paul's day, the public reading of Scripture was more important than today, as books were scarce and costly and the people were often illiterate, so that knowledge of the Scriptures was gained by these public readings.

Yet, this practice is of vital importance today also for the Scriptures are the only infallible word from God we have today. However inspiring a sermon may be, only the Scriptures are "inspired" in the sense of inerrantly communicating the mind and will of God. In fact, the preaching that takes place is an exposition of the passage read. So, it is important to place this passage before the people prior to expounding it.

We are reminded that public reading in the ancient world called for some technical accomplishment. This is because the letters, all in capitals, were lumped together without spaces dividing the words in the following manner:

NOSPACESDIVIDINGTHEWORDS.

Today reading is much easier. Yet public reading today also calls for some skill because, even though reading is easier, people find it more difficult to listen. They are so used to receiving audiovisual messages involving both sight and sound through the media, such as television, that they find it difficult to concentrate when a person simply reads.

We need to capture the attention of our hearers with lively reading. A brief introduction to the passage may help prepare the listener by attracting his attention. The reader must attempt to catch the mood of the passage and communicate its feeling so that the hearers will enter into the experience that lies behind the lesson. This is not to be confused with a "theatrical performance," which may impress the hearer but leave him cold. What is being read is the "living and active" Word of God, which is "sharper than any double-edged sword" (Heb. 4:12). The reading needs to reflect to the hearers this potency of the Word.

The challenge to better public reading calls for certain safeguards. We must be careful in choosing readers. Very often we give the job to a person who is not a good reader. There is evidence to suggest that in the early church there was a special office of reader (or lector) open to "educated and trained" persons (Ralph Martin, *Worship in the Early Church,* London: Morgan and Scott, 1972). The reader also should prayerfully and carefully prepare for his reading, even if it is assigned to him just a few minutes before the meeting begins.

PERSONAL APPLICATION

Do a spiritual inventory with your life, beliefs, and ministry, using the six features of a model ministry learned in this lesson. Spend as much time on it as you can. Try to cover as many areas of your life, beliefs, and ministry as you can. Ask, "How am I faring in my devotional life, in my reading, and so on?"

ELEVEN
THE LEADER'S
RELATIONSHIPS (5:1-16)

We have already alluded to the fact that relationships are a very important aspect of Christian leadership. It is not surprising, then, that Paul's book of instructions to the young leader, Timothy, has more than a whole chapter devoted to the topic of relationships with various classes of people in the Christian community (5:1–6:2).

RELATING TO OLDER MEN (5:1a)

The first class of people mentioned are older men. Paul said, "Do not rebuke an older man harshly, but exhort him as if he were your father" (5:1a).

In biblical times the change from maturity to old age was considered to have taken place at sixty years. Old people were held in honor for their experience and wisdom. Old age was not a thing to be ashamed of as Proverbs shows: "Gray hair [is] the splendor of the old" (20:29). Gray hair was a mark of honor! The Bible also asks us to show respect for age. Leviticus 19:32 says, "Rise in the presence of the aged, show respect for the elderly." Isaiah shows part of the symptoms of Israel's ill health as disrespect for the elderly (3:5).

If the Bible advocates such an attitude of respect toward elders how must a young leader like Timothy respond when an older person does wrong? Certainly he must not ignore the error, nor "rebuke [him] harshly," but exhort him as if he were his father.

The word translated "exhort" *(parakaleo)* originally meant to call aside, either to encourage, comfort, exhort, or admonish. So this word takes different meanings according to the context in which it is used. The idea of admonition is predominant in the verse we are discussing. The young leader calls the erring older person and admonishes him, but as a son—not as a superior. He does it with respect and affection.

When an elder, who is a sincere person, is admonished in this way, he will realize that the correction comes not from a desire to throw one's weight around but from a just and honorable motive. So he will take the leader's word seriously and without dismissing it as one of the zealous excesses of an inexperienced young upstart.

D. L. Moody and his wife, Emma, were a good example of admonition. Emma was the well-educated daughter of a rich businessman. Moody had had very little education and came from a poor family. Emma had a big part to play in educating Moody for his public ministry. Emma corrected his grammar and his spelling and his grooming and a dozen other things. But, as Ethel Barrett says, "she did it with such charm and in such love that he never knew he was being criticized" *(Will the Real Phony Please Stand Up,* Regal Books, 1969). At the end of his life Moody was said to say that he never ceased to be astonished that God gave him such a great ministry, and that God gave him his wife.

While the details of Moody and his wife do not apply to the verse we are studying, their example shows us the type of attitude that should be seen when a leader corrects a person who is socially his senior. It should be an attitude of humility, respect, and affection mingled with a passion for truth and righteousness.

RELATING TO YOUNGER MEN (5:1b)

Paul then said, "Treat younger men as brothers." This remark could be interpreted in one of two ways. Paul may still have been continuing on the theme of exhorting different classes of wrongdoers. Or he may have moved on to Timothy's day-to-day relationships with other classes of people. In either case, the message that comes out of both interpretations points to the attitudes that should characterize our relationships with different classes of people.

Paul was to regard young men as brothers. Even though there are differences in office within the church, all Christians are of equal status before God. This did not mean that Timothy was to relinquish his leadership role. His friendship with his fellows was not to hinder him from leading them. But as a leader he did not need to put on airs or try to act unnaturally with people his own age, attempting to lord it over them.

RELATING TO OLDER WOMEN (5:2a)

Paul again reminded Timothy of the need to respect age: "Treat . . . older women as mothers" (5:2).

These three directives remind us that while leaders do have an authority (actually a derived authority) they must exercise it prudently, humbly, and sensitively.

RELATING TO YOUNGER WOMEN (5:2b)

The fourth class of people Paul mentioned was younger women: "Treat . . . younger women as sisters" (5:2b). Paul then took the opportunity to slip in a quiet warning by adding ". . . with absolute purity." The best of leaders can err in their relationships with members of the opposite sex. The writer of Proverbs vividly explains how hard it is to predict what can happen when a man is with a woman: "There are three things that are too amazing for me, four that I do not understand: the way of an eagle in the sky, the way of a snake on a rock, the way of a ship on the high seas, and the way of a man with a maiden" (Prov. 30:18, 19).

This directive by Paul did not mean that, because of the potential dangers, Timothy was to avoid contacts with Christians of the opposite sex. Leadership responsibilities make such contacts necessary. But Timothy's contacts were to be characterized by "absolute purity."

Paul had used the word "purity" earlier in 4:12 to describe the example Timothy was to set. In 5:2 he strengthened the force of what he was saying by adding the adjective "all" or "absolute." In our discussion of 4:12 we said that the word "purity" carried the dual emphases of moral purity and of integrity of motive. In dealing with members of the opposite sex, a leader's outward actions must be pure and his inner motives must be unmixed.

Sometimes, in a relationship of this nature, one's motives could get mixed along the way. What began as an innocent counseling appointment may develop into a relationship with an unhealthy emotional content to it, a condition that is not fully recognized until it has gone too far. For this reason, a leader needs to be extremely careful in this area. When an unhealthy tinge is detected by the leader himself or by a discerning friend, it must be dealt with at once.

Some people in this situation will try to claim that their case is the exception to the rule. But such people are treading on dangerous ground. As an American Methodist bishop once pointed out, the story of the church is tainted with numerous examples of the fall of ministers who presumed that they were the exception to the rule in the area of relationships with the opposite sex.

THE WELFARE OF WIDOWS (5:3-16)

We next come to a surprisingly long section about the welfare of widows (5:3-16). It indicates the concern the early church had toward the less privileged. This type of person could be easily overlooked while the church was busy going about its other activities, as had earlier happened in the Jerusalem church. That church had to develop a system by which they could ensure that the needy were looked after (Acts 6). Such a system had been developed in the church in Ephesus, too. Paul gave Timothy some guidelines for administering such a system because as leader of the church Timothy was responsible for seeing that the task was being done properly.

Finding the Truly Needy (5:3-8). Paul said, "Give proper recognition [or support] to those widows who are really in need" (v. 3). The next few verses give guidelines on how to find out who such ones really are. Some aid schemes today are too mechanical and simple. An example would be a scheme which says something to the effect that all widows must be given a certain amount of money each month. Half those widows may not need any assistance at all. The other half may need more than the amount prescribed. Other schemes are haphazard, sometimes depending entirely on the mood and the feelings of the administering officer. Under such a haphazard scheme, the truly needy people often get nothing at all. Anyone given such a responsibility of aiding needy people must develop some clear guidelines to find out who really needs assistance and how much.

Paul eliminated those who could get help from their family members (v. 4). He then gave them three suggestions as to how one may recognize a truly needy widow (v. 5). First, she has been "left all alone," with no family to support her. Second, she "puts her hope in God," which seems to suggest that, because she has no one else to help her, she has to look to God and his people for assistance. Third, she "continues night and day to pray and to ask God for help." Like Anna the prophetess, she is a woman of prayer (see Luke 2:37).

Even though these widows may be old, weak, unable to support themselves and seemingly useless to the church, they still can do that work (yes it is work!), behind which lies the power of the church. They can pray! And only in heaven will we fully know how important an activity prayer was on earth. So these "weak" people have a vitally important role in the church. They are like the batteries of a torch—inside, unrecognized, but the source of power! Dare we, then, despise the aged? Dare we laugh at the "little old ladies" of the women's missionary society?

After those lofty thoughts about widows who are devoted to incessant prayer, Paul came down to earth by talking about another type of widow whose devotion is to incessant "pleasure" (5:6). These worldly-minded, self-indulgent widows didn't qualify for the church's assistance.

Next Paul asked Timothy to explain these principles to the church "so that no one may be open to blame" (5:7). If the principles are known by all and carefully carried out, then there will be no murmuring in the church about unworthy people being assisted while worthy people go without assistance.

An Order of Widows (5:9-10). Paul seemed to be talking about those belonging to an order of widows that had been established in the Ephesian church (v. 9). This church not only developed a structure for giving assistance to the aged, it also found a means by which those widows who desired to serve God could do so.

Due to our "achievement mentality," we often dismiss older

people as useless because they cannot produce according to our
ideas of achievement. In this we Christians have simply adopted
the false values of a society that worships youth and despises old
age. Not so in the traditional Eastern society, where older people
had a place of high honor.

God has planned the structure of the church in such a way that
for true progress both young and old need to participate actively.
The Bible clearly teaches that everyone is significant in the body
of Christ because they all have a unique part to play in the progress
of the body (1 Cor. 12). This body includes old people, too. Part of
a leader's responsibility is to discover what service God has
planned for the elderly and provide a structure by which they could
fulfill this plan of God for their lives.

Now not everyone could enter this order. Strict standards have
always been maintained for all official positions in the church. The
order of widows was no exception. So Paul gave some qualifications to determine who was to be admitted to the order:

*No widow may be put on the list of widows unless she is over sixty,
has been faithful to her husband, and is well known for her good
deeds, such as bringing up children, showing hospitality, washing
the feet of the saints, helping those in trouble and devoting herself to
all kinds of good deeds (vv. 9, 10).*

A point that comes out clearly in this list of qualities is the
unselfishness of those who were admitted to the order. Some
widows get into a shell after losing their life partner and never
come out of it. Indeed, losing one's mate could be the most
traumatic experience one encounters in life, as numerous surveys
have shown. And I am not going to attempt to provide solutions
to this difficult problem here. I will only say that surely an
important aspect of the solution would be in finding a place of
service, an opportunity to give oneself in helping others. Then the
widow will realize her useful life is not over. She has a significant
role to play in the service of her Master. And she will give herself
to this role.

Younger Widows (5:11-15). In the following passage, verses 11-15,
we see Paul's realism. Knowing the makeup of younger women, he
showed that it was unfair and unwise to make demands

of them that are unnatural to their physical desires. So the order of widows was open only for those over sixty. The younger widows were counseled to remarry (5:14). To remain single was to open themselves to unnecessary temptation.

One would wish this wise realism were seen in all the Christian movements that place high emphasis on community living. Often in these communities young men and women, having answered a call to a "higher life" which includes singleness, participate in a special kind of community life and service. The sad stories of moral lapses in such communities would warn us to be careful about legislating celibacy for the young and the middle-aged who want to serve God in a special way.

CARING FOR AGED FAMILY MEMBERS (4:4, 8, 16)

Three verses in this section are devoted to showing the need for relatives to look after aged family members. Paul used some very strong language to drive home his point. (a) In verse 4 he said, "But if a widow has children or grandchildren, these should learn first of all to put their religion into practice by caring for their own family." (b) Paul regarded such care as an act of "repaying their parents and grandparents." (c) Then he said that "this is pleasing to God." (d) In verse 8 his language got even stronger: "If anyone does not provide for his relatives, and especially for his immediate family, he has denied the faith and is worse than an unbeliever." (e) Verse 16 says, "If any woman who is a believer has widows in her family, she should help them and not let the church be burdened with them." (f) One reason why this is so important is that then "the church can help those widows who are really in need."

Six important propositions are made here, and each one has much to say to contemporary society. Caring for aged parents has been a normal practice over the past generations. But in recent years it is not considered as natural a thing as it was before, because it involves too much trouble and often goes against one's personal goals. When children make decisions about career and employment today rarely does the calling to care for parents figure prominently in the decision making process.

Often this type of care for parents involves suffering. Yet the desire to avoid suffering cannot be a reason for abandoning one's responsibilities. Suffering is woven into the fabric of life in this fallen world. The Christian way of love invariably brings with it a cup of suffering. Are we not following a suffering Savior who called us to give our lives for others as he did (John 15:12-14)? Have we not been told that the sovereign Lord uses suffering to mediate some deep work for good in our lives (James 1:2-4)? So we will not try to avoid the suffering that comes from devotion to duty. We will face it in anticipation of God's provision and sovereign work for good through it.

An issue related to the topic of the Christian's call to look after parents is the responsibility of converts to Christianity from other faiths towards their families. Most parents of converts resent the fact that their children have discarded the family religion, unless they too have come to Christ, which has happened often. One of their biggest fears is that the converted children will not carry out the family responsibilities. Often this fear is not unfounded. The converts' lives begin to revolve so much around their newfound spiritual family that they begin to neglect their physical families. I believe Paul's words about betraying Christ apply to these also, for they dishonor Christ by their lack of concern for their families. Should we not encourage Christian boys, for instance, to delay marriage, if necessary, in order to provide for their sisters' marriages? Would that not be an extension of the principle of repaying parents (5:4)?

A helpful illustration comes from the experience of a convert from a devout Brahmin family in India, who became a Christian evangelist. He was ostracized by his family. For years they had nothing to do with him. Then his father died. In keeping with an accepted Brahmin custom, the evangelist began to send regular financial support to his widowed mother. She received the support, but refused to establish contact with him. This went on for six years. Finally contact was reestablished. When this happened, the evangelist exhibited more and more willingness to take on the responsibility for his mother's welfare. Today she is proud of his concern and the door has been opened for a Christian witness to the whole family.

Paul's words have reminded us of the importance of relationships in the work of Christian leadership. Christianity is a community religion. And communities exist on relationships. When relationships break, communities break. So however talented a leader may be, if he does not work on his relationships, he will not be effective.

PERSONAL APPLICATION

Evaluate your relationship with each of the six groups of people mentioned in this study. Write down any concrete changes you may need to make in these relationships.

TWELVE
SUPERVISING
LEADERS (5:17–25)

Paul gave to Timothy more specific instructions on how to relate to different classes of people in the church. Continuing with the theme of instructions about relationships, he moved on to one of the most delicate relationships Timothy had to face—his relationship with the highest level of leaders in the church, the elders (5:17-25).

PAYMENT FOR WORKERS (5:17, 18)

Paul first tackled the matter of payment for elders: "The elders who direct the affairs of the church well are worthy of double honor, especially those whose work is preaching and teaching" (5:17). The word "honor" and the word "recognition" used in verse 3 are the same Greek word. In verse 3 it was used in connection with payments for widows. Paul said here that elders "are worthy of double honor." This does not mean they are to be paid double, but that they should be given enough so that they can be free to concentrate on their ministries.

To substantiate his point, Paul used two quotations from "Scripture" (5:19). The first was from Deuteronomy 25:4: "Do not muzzle the ox while it is treading out the grain." This was a command made out of consideration for cattle. The farmers were to allow them to take an occasional bite as they worked on treading grain. The second quotation was from the words of Jesus: "The

worker deserves his wages." This is the first time the words of
Jesus are described as being part of Scripture. Probably there
were collections of the words of Jesus being circulated at that
time, and the church regarded them as bearing God's authority,
just as the Old Testament Scriptures did.

Paul wanted to make sure that the church did not take advantage
of Christian workers who had given up regular employment in
order to devote themselves to Christian work. It is a clear evidence that there was a paid ministry in the early church. Earlier
Paul had said that those with a love for money should be disqual-
ified from the ministry (3:3). He deplored Christian workers being
exploited by the church that didn't give them adequate remuneration.

In many places of the world, there seems to be two extreme
types of payment for Christian workers with only a few in between.
On the one hand, there are ministers of many churches and
organizations who are grossly underpaid and whose ministry is
hindered by their various financial burdens. On the other hand,
there are those who are paid very high salaries.

I believe that the poor salaries given to our ministers are a grave
sign of ill health in the Christian community. It could be a sign of
the church's lack of concern for the welfare of its workers. It could
be a sign of the failure of the church to nurture Christians who
have learned to give scripturally. It could also be a sign of the
church's lack of enthusiasm over the quality of ministry coming
from its workers. Of course, the cycle is vicious. If the church is
unjust in the way it pays its workers, it would not be surprising if
these workers became demotivated due to being unjustly treated
and as a result, began to perform low-quality ministry.

The main point Paul was making in these verses was that
ministers should be freed from financial burdens so that they could
concentrate on their ministries. The church should take it on as its
responsibility to ensure that this happens.

Having said this, we will add that for the sake of an effective
witness among the poor, some Christian workers may be called to
relative poverty. In Sri Lanka, for example, a large percentage of
our people are poor. Since Christianity has made such little inroad
among the poor, many Christian workers may be called to a
simpler life-style than is considered normal by the average Christian.

We must also bear in mind that to the average Buddhist and to many Hindus, simplicity is considered a necessary part of piety. An extravagant life-style would seriously affect our credibility and close the door to our witness to them. Of course, there are some poor non-Christians who are attracted to Christian churches that appear wealthy because they feel that some of that wealth could come to them. Alas, many so-called conversions to Christ that have taken place in recent and past history in some places have been instances of people coming to grab the economic assistance that would come to them if they became Christians. These people are so-called rice Christians, not followers of Christ.

PREACHING AND TEACHING AS KEYS TO LEADERSHIP (5:17)

Paul makes an interesting allusion to the place the preaching and teaching ministries have in directing the church. Paul seemed to say that "the elders who direct the affairs of the church" are "especially those whose work is preaching and teaching" (v. 17). I believe we are correct in implying from this that preaching and teaching are the primary forces in directing the church. For this reason the apostles in the Jerusalem church needed to be set apart from other duties for the sake of their ministry of prayer and the Word (Acts 6:2, 4).

God is the ultimate leader of the people of God. If so, they must be led primarily by the Word of God. The human leader who directs this group has the responsibility of communicating this Word to the people. In order to do this accurately he needs to spend time with God, in prayer and in the Word. Only then could he adequately represent God, the real Leader of the people.

Christian leadership, then, is essentially done through the communication of the will of God to God's people. This in turn is done mainly through the ministries of preaching and teaching. So a leader's chief task is to preach and teach.

Today there seems to be a trend in a different direction in the church. Joseph Bayly records this trend thus: "Managers and administrators seem to be replacing pioneers and leaders in our Christian organizations. This carry-over from American business is accompanied by other similar accommodations" ("The How-to Church," *Eternity,* January, 1983, p. 15). This new trend places the primary emphasis in leadership upon management and administration, and not upon the ministry of the Word. So the major responsibilities of a bishop or president of a church or the director of a Christian organization are administrative. His primary skills must be in managing the organization. Directing the people into a realization of the word God has for them is a secondary function in his leadership role.

Indeed, it is essential for all leaders to develop management skills. But if that becomes the major function of leadership, the church or the Christian organization will become like a secular organization. It will not move forward under the voice of God into new exploits for the kingdom. It will lose its prophetic role with its distinct word from God for our generation if the leadership gives a low priority to the work of hearing from the Word of God and communicating it to the church.

WHEN A LEADER SINS (5:19-21)

After dealing with the payment of elders, Paul moved on to the topic of reproving elders: "Do not entertain an accusation against an elder unless it is brought by two or three witnesses." Leaders must not be at the mercy of some evil-minded person who decides to accuse them for wrongdoing.

Because the decisions and actions of leaders affect a large number of people, they have ample occasion to rub people the wrong way. If a leader has disciplined someone, or made a decision which someone does not like, that person could have angry feelings toward the leader. Such feelings could cause his judgments and opinions about the leader to be quite inaccurate. Even an honest and good person could be swayed, because of personal ill feeling toward another, into misinterpreting his actions and arriving at wrong judgments about him. Leaders are particularly open to such misunderstandings, due to a natural bias against leadership so common today.

With such possibilities for false accusations, Paul counseled Timothy not to take action on an accusation until he was sure of the facts. The best way to be sure is to have several independent witnesses who will attest to the wrongdoing.

If, however, the accusation is proved to be true, Timothy was not to try to hush it up. "Those who sin are to be rebuked publicly

so that the others may take warning" (5:20). I must confess that
this was to me the most jolting and troubling statement in this
whole epistle. It gives evidence of the passionate hatred leaders
need to have for things that dishonor God. Some commentators
have reduced the force of this statement by interpreting the word
"publicly" to mean only in front of the elders. But this seems to be
unnatural to the context. Paul seems to be suggesting full exposure before the church.

Leaders are to be examples to God's people of the beauty of
virtue. But when they fail, they become examples of the ugliness
of sin. So when a leader sins, it becomes a very serious concern
for the church. The church must face up squarely to the fact that
the one who was expected to be a model of godliness has become
just the opposite, so he must be rebuked in front of those to
whom he was a poor example. What an awesome responsibility
leadership is!

In the second part of this verse Paul gave the positive result for
the church of leaders being rebuked publicly: "Others . . . take
warning." Others in the church will realize that if a leader can fall
into sin and be punished, it could happen to them, too. They could
also see how sin committed by leaders dishonors God. They would
be warned that the church does not condone sin. They would
understand that if they want to remain associated with the people
of God, they would have to flee evil. They would also be warned
that they too may be humiliated as the leader was if they sinned
like he did. Fear of punishment seems a very lowly motive for
holiness, but, considering human nature, we sometimes need such
jolting truths to keep us from yielding to temptation.

Paul gave a solemn charge to Timothy: "I charge you, in the
sight of God and Christ Jesus and the elect angels, to keep these
instructions without partiality and to do nothing out of favoritism"
(v. 21). Paul had just asked Timothy to do something he would
have shrunk from doing, considering his timid nature—disciplining
sinning elders. So Paul included a solemn charge to impress upon
him the need to fulfill this unpleasant task with careful consistency.
If Timothy failed here, he would open the door to ruining the
church; to letting it slip into becoming an insipid organization
without the fire of God's holiness in it.

In these matters of church discipline, Timothy was to act
"without partiality." The Greek word used here *(prokrima)* literally

means prejudgment, so it could be translated as "prejudice." Timothy was not to admit doubtful charges against a person without proper investigation simply because he did not like that person. How easy it is to believe bad things said about people we don't like!

Next Paul said, "Do nothing out of favoritism." The word used here *(proklisis)* literally means "inclination." There are certain people toward whom we are naturally drawn or inclined. When a charge brought against them is proved true, we may excuse their wrongdoing or be lenient with them because we like them, which is favoritism at its worst. We all have the tendency to put different people into good and bad categories. When good people do things wrong, we give excuses for them. When bad people do good things, we tend to attribute ulterior motives to them.

Leaders cannot help liking some people and disliking others. But they must make sure that these likes and dislikes, these preferences and prejudices, do not influence their actions as leaders. This is particularly important because the church takes such a hard stand on sin. If there is no consistency here, all sorts of injustices and abuses could result.

CHOOSING LEADERS (5:22-25)

Continuing on the theme of supervising elders, Paul said, "Do not be hasty in the laying on of hands" (5:22a). He was referring here to the ceremony of ordaining people into leadership positions by laying hands on them. Timothy was not to be in a hurry to appoint leaders. He was to do a thorough investigation of the person before making the appointment. Once the person was appointed, it would be very difficult and unpleasant to drop him from leadership if he proved to be unsuitable, though sometimes that had to be done. But a lot of damage would be done before this happened. It would have been far better to have been slow in making the appointment.

Paul continued, "Do not share in the sins of others," referring to the personal responsibility the leader had when he appointed someone to an office in the church. If Timothy appointed someone, he became responsible for the choice, and in some way responsible for the person's behavior and any sins that the person might commit. He could not simply wash his hands of the situation. He would have to share in the scandal. How careful he needed to be when appointing leaders!

A lot of Christian work today is done by using what may be called the "project system" of operation. A project proposal is presented to a donor agency. It is approved by the agency and the money for it is sent. Sometimes the donor agency itself decides what the project is and sends money with instructions on how it should be spent.

Once the money is sent, it is essential that the project should get underway without delay. But often there are no suitable people to do the job, and the wrong people are appointed. Because the method and the techniques used were effective, the project was a success as far as statistics are concerned. But what about the heavenly perspective? A lot of this work would prove to be of a wood, hay, and stubble quality when the fires of God's judgment are applied to it (1 Cor. 3:12). Because it was done out of the wrong motives, by the wrong people, it does not have God's approval.

We often hear people say that money is the key to world evangelization. If only we had enough money, they say, we could reach the whole world for Christ. Sometimes, however, as in the above cases, money is a curse and not a key. Dedicated workers are the key. I believe it is often well worth waiting—even holding back progress—until God provides such workers.

Paul's next word to Timothy was, "Keep yourself pure" (5:22c). Did Paul mean, keep yourself pure by making the right choice of leaders? Possibly. But, more probably, he meant to impress upon Timothy the fact that as the key leader it was very important for him to be pure. Indeed, Timothy must appoint pure workers. But, even more important, as far as Timothy was concerned, was the need for him to keep himself pure.

Three times in this book the word "pure" has appeared in connection with the leader's life-style (see 4:12 and 5:2). As we have said before, this word carries the dual idea of moral purity and integrity of motive. Only as Timothy was pure would he be consistent in enforcing high standards on other leaders in the church. Only then would he be qualified to rebuke and discipline others who had sinned. If the church was to have dedicated people in positions of responsibility, its key leaders would have to set the standard of total dedication to Christ. If such dedication was missing, the poison would gradually spread like gangrene throughout the whole body, causing spiritual bankruptcy in the community.

Paul included an unusual personal note about Timothy's health. This reference to Timothy's health is so typical of Paul and a strong argument in support of the fact that it was Paul who wrote this letter. He said, "Stop drinking only water, and use a little wine because of your stomach and your frequent illness" (v. 23). Paul had just asked Timothy to keep himself pure. But this did not mean that Timothy had to neglect his physical health as the ascetic heretics in Ephesus did.

The physical side of a person was not evil, as these false teachers claimed. The body has its needs, so Timothy was to look after it. He was a person of delicate health, and wine was believed to be good for his health. Earlier, Paul had said that bodily exercise was of little value whereas godliness was of great value (4:8). There he was asking Timothy to get his priorities straight. Yet this did not mean that Timothy was to neglect the physical side of his life.

Paul returned to the topic of forming a right estimate of people. Paul said that "the sins of some are obvious, reaching the place of judgment ahead of them; the sins of others trail behind them" (v. 24). Some people are so flagrant in their sinfulness that everyone knows what the outcome will be when they go before the judgment. The sins of other people are less obvious. They trail behind them and cannot be detected at first. But these sins will finally catch up with them at the judgment.

A person who faithfully attends meetings and gives every indication of being a devout Christian may be dishonest at work, unkind at home, or unreliable with money. These sins surface only after careful investigation. Because of this, Timothy was not to be hasty in placing a person in a leadership position. He was first to make every effort to find out what type of person was being chosen for the position.

Just as a person's sins may not be apparent on the surface, so also his goodness may not be immediately apparent (v. 25), so a good leader looks carefully for the right qualities in people.

All through this study, I was constantly struck by what an awesome responsibility leading God's people is. Leadership is not something to take lightly. Leadership is not a position open and available to everyone. Only the spiritually qualified can assume the role. To drop our standards here is to open the door to ruin within the church.

PERSONAL APPLICATION

1. Are the full-time workers in your church or organization adequately paid? If not, what should you do about it? Lay leaders must consider it an important responsibility to ensure that workers are adequately paid.

2. Is the direction of your church or organization primarily based on the ministry of the Word or upon some other philosophy? If not based on the ministry of the Word, what can you do to bring back the biblical perspective to leadership?

THIRTEEN
THE CHRISTIAN ATTITUDE TOWARD POSSESSIONS
(6:5b–10)

One great advantage of going through a book of the Bible when studying a particular topic is that themes not usually considered in such a study emerge unexpectedly and demand consideration. We would not usually consider the theme of one's attitude toward possessions in a course on leadership. Yet this theme figures prominently in 1 Timothy.

Experience tells us that the theme of one's attitude toward possessions is important to any discussion of leadership because one's attitude to material things has a big influence on one's relationship with God. We all know of Christians who were all out for God in their youth who became quite lukewarm in their commitment as they grew older. A major cause for this slide was an unchristian attitude toward possessions. Those hoping to lead younger Christians into maturity should, early in the discipling relationship, give some instruction on the Christian attitude toward possessions. In fact, Christian leaders themselves need to constantly be on their guard to ensure that they don't veer away from God's will for their lives in this area. So, we do not apologize for considering this theme in a book on leadership life-style.

RELIGION AS A MEANS OF FINANCIAL GAIN (6:5)

Paul gave Timothy yet another warning about false teachers. He exposed the evil character and schemes of these teachers and concluded by saying that "they think that godliness is a means to financial gain" (6:5).

Most scholars think it unlikely that this statement means these teachers preached that Christianity was a means of getting rich. Today we hear preachers calling people to come to Christ and become rich by doing so. But in the early church there were few opportunities for Christians to get rich quick. It was more probable that these false teachers were using their ministry as a means of earning money. They may have charged high fees for their teaching on "godliness," as other philosophical teachers of the day did.

Although we see that Paul in his epistles insisted on full-time Christian workers being given adequate remuneration (see 1 Cor. 9:7-14; 1 Tim. 5:17, 18), he disapproved of leaving room for giving the world the impression that Christians were using the ministry to make money. Such practices would dishonor Christ and cheapen the gospel. He himself, in certain places, refused to take any financial support for his services, even though he had a right to do so and even when the people were willing to help him. Instead, he earned his living by making tents (see 1 Cor. 9:12, 15; 1 Thess. 2:3-10). Paul wanted to be doubly careful in this area, but yet he encouraged churches to pay their workers adequately. These workers, however, must never use money as a criterion for ministry. In fact, Paul insisted that "a lover of money" should not be appointed to the ministry (1 Tim. 3:3).

As we apply Paul's statement to today's church, I suppose the first thought that comes to us is of evangelists who have manipulated people and have used their preaching gift to become rich. Thank God for men like Billy Graham who, by their scrupulous financial dealings, have preserved the good name of the office of evangelist. In certain places in the world, the offerings rarely suffice to even cover expenses. But evangelists often get rich through gifts from foreign donors. Their high income allows them to live on a much higher economic level than those to whom they minister, a practice Paul would surely have opposed.

This verse also reminds me of the famous Christian preachers and lecturers who, in keeping with the practice in society, have fixed fees for their "appearances." The more famous the preacher, the higher the fee. Of course, such lecturers effectively eliminate the poor from benefitting from their wisdom. Poor churches could not afford to pay such high fees. The Bible says we are to have a special concern for the poor. Would that not mean that at least some of our best preachers should be ministering to those in poor neighborhoods as evangelists and pastors? But good preachers have to climb! And to minister to such people would be to come down on the ecclesiastical (and monetary) ladder.

Alas, just as the false teachers in Paul's time adopted the pagan system of levying fees for their ministry, many evangelical preachers have adopted the same pagan ideas of success in ministry. Their idea of success has been too closely linked to monetary considerations.

GODLINESS AND CONTENTMENT (6:6)

Having talked about a wrong type of gain from ministry (that is, financial gain), Paul went on to describe what a Christian should consider as real gain: "But godliness with contentment is great gain" (6:6). Note the combination of godliness and contentment, which we don't always find existing together. It is not uncommon to find "godly" people who are discontent. About such people we can make, from Paul's statement, the implication: Godliness without contentment is a great loss.

Godliness without Contentment. A person has a price to pay for choosing the path of godliness. Christ called that price "the cross" (Matt. 10:38; 16:24; Mark 8:34; Luke 9:23; 14:27). Some who decide to pay this price are unhappy about the consequences of that decision. The cross takes different forms for different Christians. It may take the form of tiredness, or poverty, or unpopularity, or persecution, or lack of free time, or failure in business due to the refusal to use unchristian methods. If a Christian resents the cross, discontentment results. This combination of "godliness" with discontentment, seen in people who are obedient to many of God's principles but unhappy about the consequences of doing so, is a great loss to the Kingdom of God.

These obedient but unhappy people communicate to the world the idea that the godly are to be pitied. People who observe them are impressed by their devotion to duty, but are not attracted to the form of godliness they practice. They see godliness as the cause for an unfulfilled life. But the life Jesus gives, which only the godly experience, is "life . . . to the full" (John 10:10). Such a full life must include fulfillment and contentment. If so-called godly people are discontented and unfulfilled, it is because some essential ingredient of biblical godliness is missing from their lives.

Discontentment is one reason for the so-called "rebellious children of the parsonage." Children often hear their discontented ministering parents grumble about the problems they are facing because of the ministry. They may grumble about the low salary they receive, or about a father or mother who is away from home for long periods on ministry activity, or about the lack of privacy because of the many people who visit their home. The children begin to resent the religion that has caused such unhappiness in their lives. Their next step may be to rebel against the God of this religion.

Discontentment also has a bad effect on fellow Christians. Paul said elsewhere that when one member of the body suffers everyone else suffers with him (1 Cor. 12:26). Because of the nature of Christian body life, when one member is discontented, gloom spreads through the whole body to take away their Christian joy. The unrest becomes all the more acute if the discontented person is a faithful, hardworking, godly person, because such a person would be an important contributor to the inner life of the community.

So, godliness without contentment is a great loss. But godliness combined with contentment is a great gain, as it reflects in an unmistakable way the beauty of God's plan for man. It tells the world that the life Christ gives is abundant and fulfilling. It powerfully challenges the hedonist who says that to truly enjoy life it is necessary to indulge in what the Christians call sin. Believers are encouraged in their walk with God. Unbelievers are challenged to consider Christ. And God is glorified.

The Nature of Contentment. What does Christian contentment mean? Often contentment arises from one's lot in life. In fact, sometimes even godliness is spoken of as being directly related to one's lot. So we hear statements like, "Give him a little prominence and he will serve the church faithfully and happily," or "Once she is cured of her sickness, she will return to the Lord and be happy once more in the Christian fellowship." But such godliness and contentment depend on causes which are too uncertain. If the causes were taken away, first the contentment goes and later even the godliness may go away.

The Greek word Paul uses for contentment *(autarkeia)* originally carried the idea of self-sufficiency or self-mastery. This quality was held high by the Stoic philosophers in Paul's time. They sought to be so much in control of themselves that they would rigidly accept whatever experiences they had to face.

The Christian idea has some similarities to the Stoic idea of self-mastery. Paul said:

I have learned to be content whatever the circumstances. I know what it is to be in need, and I know what it is to have plenty. I have learned the secret of being content in any and every situation, whether well fed or hungry, whether living in plenty or in want (Phil. 4:11, 12).

The Christian concept, however, adds the idea of joyous contentment to the Greek idea of self-mastery. The Christian believes that a good God is in control of his life. In every situation this good God works for the good of those who love him (Rom. 8:28). Therefore, the Christian is happy with his lot. He knows that in every circumstance God is working out his purposes. So, Christian contentment is more than a Stoic self-mastery. It is a joyous acceptance of every situation of life.

The Stoics accepted situations with a determined resolution to master them. There are others who accept situations with a fatalistic resignation. When there is a bad turn of fortune, they say, "What can I do? It has happened. Now I will have to learn to live with it." A Hindu may say, "It is my karma," or "It is my fate," or "It is the will of Shiva." A Muslim might say, "It is the will of Allah."

Not so the Christian. He bases his living on the premise that a good and loving God controls his life. We are masters of circumstances because he is master of everything. When this truth hits us, it liberates us from anxiety and discontent. So, our contentment is essentially contentment in him.

When difficulties come, our view of him may become temporarily blocked by clouds of doubt. Then we become discontent. But as we take hold of the numerous promises in God's Word and let the Holy Spirit apply them to our lives, the light of God's providence shines through. We see things as they really are. God is sovereign over history. He is good. I am his child. He has promised to look after me. So he will do something wonderful through my situation.

When a Christian faces a difficult situation, he is able to face it, not merely with a grim determination, not merely with a fatalistic resignation over the inevitable, but with a joyous hope in the Master of all situations, our loving Father.

Contentment and Injustice. If a Christian is to be contented with his lot and assured that God is working some good out of it, is it wrong for him to be dissatisfied over situations that need to be changed? Does his contentment lull him to a passive acceptance of injustice and inequality? If so, Karl Marx would be right in his assessment that religion is the opiate of the masses. But this is far from correct.

Christian contentment is part of an active Christian life. It is inseparably linked with obedience to God. A part of Christian obedience is the call of God to restore his glory in a world marred by sin. Since injustice is one of these sins, the Christian battles it. Rather than being an opiate, Christianity is a motivating force to our being involved in changing situations, spiritual or material, which do not conform to God's will. In fact, if a Christian refuses to be involved in such work, he will lose his contentment. Paul, for example, was very restless when he was not about the work of battling unbelief (see Acts 17:16, 17; 1 Cor. 9:16).

With that background, we are in a position to ask a more tricky question. We agree that Christians need to battle for the rights of the oppressed, but what if we are the ones who are being wronged? For example, is it right for a church worker to complain about his salary?

A look at Paul's life shows that he did at times protest about injustices committed against him. At Philippi he made known to the officials that they had wronged him and asked for some redress (Acts 16:37-39). In the letters to the Corinthians and Galatians, we see him defending himself in the light of unjust criticisms.

Yet, observing Paul's life, we see that what ultimately motivated

him was the honor of Christ, whose representative he was.
Injustice dishonors Christ. And whether it is committed against us
or others, we will battle it because of a commitment to Christ's
honor. So when Paul defended himself before the Galatians the
issue at stake was the gospel of Christ.

Take the case of the church worker who is underpaid. This
injustice will adversely affect the health of the church. It wrongs
one of the church's key workers and so opens the door for a drop
in the quality of his service. It also makes the church guilty of the
sin of unjustly treating one of its own. Knowing how all this will
dishonor Christ, the worker will try to change the situation.

An underpaid worker in a "secular" organization has a slightly
different motivation. But he too could strive for his rightful pay.
The Christian seeks to see the lordship of Christ in the structures
of society. Since the organization for which he works is one of
these structures, he can strive to bring justice to it. Its injustice
dishonors the Creator of the society of which the organization is a
part.

Yet, when a Christian agitator fights for rights, he always keeps
before him some safeguards. First, because of his commitment to
the honor of Christ, he will stay clear of using any method that
would dishonor Christ. For example, he would not drag battles
within the church into the secular courts, which would dishonor
Christ before the world (see 1 Cor. 6:1-6). I remember, with great
shame, the court case between two groups of Protestant Christians in Sri Lanka over a church union scheme. The case was
presided over by a Muslim judge. Even though the Protestants are
less than 1 percent of the population, the case received prominent
coverage in the national newspapers.

The method the Christian uses in battling injustice reflects an
inseparable combination of justice and love. Many people think
this method is too slow in bringing about change, so they choose a
quicker method and use some unchristian means such as violence,
hatred, and revenge. But such methods, though sometimes
yielding immediate results, only add to the misery of this world,
because they go against the principles for a good society which
God, the Creator of society, set in motion.

The greatest force for good in the world today is Christian
holy-love. Mahatma Gandhi, though not a Christian, upheld

something very close to it, and he showed the world its power in influencing people in the direction of goodness. But that force is rarely used today. How we need truly Christian fighters for justice—people whose methods are all drawn from the principles of Christ!

Another safeguard for a Christian battling for justice is to never allow the injustice to become the main issue. To the Christian, the main issue is always Jesus and his glory. The Christian should be willing to endure injustice if he believes that battling over his rights will adversely affect his testimony or dishonor Christ.

The main issue in one's life ultimately colors the way he views life at any one time. He may lose his peace and become agitated over a situation on earth, as Paul did over the heresies in the Galatian church (Gal. 4:19, 20). But the peace he loses in such cases does not touch his deepest spring of peace and fulfillment, which is his relationship with God. In that same letter to the Galatians, Paul was able to speak of joy and peace as being the fruit of the Spirit's working in a person's life (Gal. 5:22).

Even though a Christian loses his peace over a situation, he must not give in to resentment. Such could happen if we lose sight of the fact that a good God is in control of our destinies, or we refuse to forgive and by so doing block the flow of God's grace into our lives, or if we reject his principles by giving in to hatred and revenge. But if we continue to trust God and his promises, then we can accept that even man's evil will be used for a good purpose by God. Joseph proclaimed such a belief to his brothers, who had mistreated him. God had used their evil devices to work out a great good that saved many lives (Gen. 50:20).

Though a Christian may be agitated over injustice, he continues to believe in God's sovereignty and to experience a live relationship with God. By doing so, he does not give in to resentment, but enjoys a contentment that is deeper and more basic to his life than the agitation over injustice.

This combination of inner peace or contentment and agitation over injustice qualifies a person to be the ideal reformer. In changing the outward unjust situations on earth such a person will not use any means that contradicts the deepest inner reality of his life, which is his relationship with God. Surely it is such a reformer—one who uses God's methods—who alone will be able to have a lasting influence for good in society.

PUTTING POSSESSIONS IN THEIR PROPER PLACE (6:7)

After talking about the importance of contentment, Paul then related contentment to the issue of material possessions, which is a common cause for discontentment in people's lives. His approach is to show us how to view the material, how to put it in its proper place: "For we brought nothing into the world, and we can take nothing out of it" (6:7).

Material possessions have only to do with this life, said Paul. We came here without them and we cannot take them with us when we leave. So, they don't have anything to do with the core of our lives.

Christ presented the same principle when he said, "Watch out! Be on your guard against all kinds of greed; a man's life does not consist in the abundance of his possessions" (Luke 12:15). Greed for the material causes discontentment. But the godly person does not have this problem because the material is not such an important feature in his life. His chief concern is with eternal realities which is what makes up his "true life." Achievement to him is primarily measured in terms of eternity.

The Christian does rejoice over material success. In fact, he may be genuinely sorry about material setbacks. The material is God's creation, so it must be taken seriously by the Christian. Yet, he does not take it so seriously that he lets its presence or absence control him.

A good way to check on our attitude about material possessions is to note our reaction when material and spiritual realities are touched. Will a father be more upset if his son forfeits an opportunity for a well-paying job or if he gets such a job but compromises a spiritual principle in telling lies at the interview? Many parents won't be upset by the compromise if the material rewards are very significant. Will a mother be more upset over her daughter being unable to find a marriage partner or over her no longer praying and reading her Bible daily?

People who depend on material things for contentment will never be truly contented, because the material is always uncertain. Since the material is not basic to life (v. 7), it needs to be put in its proper place as far as our priorities are concerned. There are other eternal realities to which we must give our fullest attention, things that are certain to provide us with an unchanging source of contentment.

WITH WHAT ARE WE TO BE CONTENT? (6:8)

Paul gave the basic material necessities with which a person is to be content: "But if we have food and clothing, we will be content with that" (v. 8). The Bible often lumps food and clothing together as minimum requirements for life (Deut. 10:18; Isa. 3:7; Matt. 6:25). The Greek word translated "clothing" means that which is necessary to cover the body, so it may include shelter also. These basic necessities God has promised to provide his children. Jesus said, "Seek first his kingdom and his righteousness, and all these things [food and clothing] will be given to you as well" (Matt. 6:33).

Sometimes, for a special purpose or mission, God may permit us to forego some basic necessities, as in a time of persecution. Sometimes poverty could be avoided, but it is accepted for the sake of some larger purpose of God, such as the honoring of his name through suffering. But these are special cases of purposeful suffering and are exceptions to the rule.

There are, however, many in the world today who are deprived of their basic necessities through no choice of their own. This we call involuntary poverty. Such poverty dishonors God and we must strive to alleviate it. We must not expect people to be satisfied with a life without the basics of food, clothing, or shelter.

What are we to do if God allows us to have something beyond our basic necessities? We will gratefully accept it as a blessing from God and seek to use it responsibly. But we will be content even if we have only the basics.

It is sad, however, that our catalogue of basics often does not tally with God's. We have a way of convincing ourselves that many luxuries are actually necessities, especially if many of our friends and neighbors have them.

When a person's estimate of his real needs and God's assessment of needs do not agree, discontentment results. Such a person is unhappy with what God has provided because he thinks it is not enough for him. He may even try to acquire more than God wills for him and may succeed in doing so. God has given man the freedom to disobey him. But no one can disobey God without losing his peace, and thus his contentment.

The idea of being content with basic necessities is not in vogue today. Success and God's blessing are often equated with material prosperity. The more we have, the more blessed we are said to be. We regard someone as being deprived and unfortunate if he does not enjoy things like running water, electricity, many outfits of clothes, color television, and car. But we must remember that when Christ, the perfect human being, lived in this world he enjoyed the bare necessities.

As Ron Sider puts it:

When God became flesh, he did not come as a wealthy Roman imperialist or a comfortable Hellenistic intellectual. He was born in an insignificant, oppressed province controlled by Imperialist Rome. Too poor to bring a lamb, the normal offering for purification, his parents brought two pigeons to the temple. Carpenters were presumably not the poorest folk in Galilean society, but they were hardly wealthy either. When he entered his public ministry, he gave up even a carpenter's comforts. (Cited in An Evangelical Commitment to Simple Life-style *by Alan Nicholas, Lausanne Committee for World Evangelism, 1980.)*

Yet Christ was a completely fulfilled person with no inhibitions or complexes. He had the wealth of inner contentment which frees a person to enjoy life fully. This is a far greater treasure than the wealth of material possessions and luxuries. So he was a complete person, receiving fulfillment from the Creator of life himself. Similarly, if our trust is in God, we too would be freed from anxiety and be able to enjoy a very contented life.

E. Stanley Jones said, "Two groups think too much about the material—those who have too much and those who have too little. We need according to our needs—we need just enough of the material so that we can forget it and get on with this business of living" (*The Word Became Flesh*, Abingdon, 1963).

THE LOVE OF MONEY (6:9, 10)

Having given principles on how to think about possessions, Paul went on to show how Christians can be led astray by wrong thinking in this area. First he referred to "people who want to get rich" (v. 9). This is indeed an apt description of many around the world, even in so-called poor nations where once wealth was available only to the elite, but is now more accessible to the poor.

As the possibility of wealth increases, so does the thirst for it.

But the thirst opens up people to the danger of compromising their principles in order to get what they want. Paul said these "people who want to get rich fall into temptation and a trap and into many foolish and harmful desires" (6:9). The words "fall" and "trap" used here show that the decline is unexpected and unplanned. When they first thirsted for wealth, they did not expect to disobey God and get into trouble spiritually. But the problem was they were walking along too treacherous a path—a path full of dangerous traps.

Among the traps into which these greedy people fall are "many foolish and harmful desires." They started with a desire to be rich which, in itself, looked harmless. But that desire led them to "harmful desires" or lusts. Lusts are desires out of control, desires not governed by principles. Paul said these lusts were "foolish," because they could not bring the satisfaction expected of them. Paul also said that they are "harmful" because they result in the destruction of people's character. Under the influence of their lust for wealth, they act in ways completely foreign to what we knew them to be.

Paul said that these desires "plunge men into ruin and destruction" (6:9c). The word translated "plunge" has the idea of submerging or drowning. Such a person has no more control over his situation. He cannot help himself.

Paul explained: "For the love of money is a root of all kinds of evil" (v. 10a). Money, which was intended to be the means of supporting life, becomes an end in itself. Money is what motivates such a person to action. Moral principles have become unimportant because making money has become more important, and all kinds of evils result. This verse does not say that every single evil comes from the love of money. But it does say that very many kinds of evil find their root in the love of money. The word "evil" is in the plural here, and would be better translated, "all kinds of evil."

Examples of the love of money leading to evil abound. There is the rampant dishonesty and the corruption that plagues nations of the so-called third world. Or consider the sin of self-centeredness when people don't find time to help others and serve God because they are so busy making money. Or consider the sin of exploitation when employers underpay workers to make more profits. Or the sin of envy and jealousy over the financial prosperity of another.

Or the evil of disharmony in families over the distribution of the family wealth.

All these are evils arising from the love of money. The desire for riches has dethroned the desire to do God's will. Mammon has become Lord. Good and bad are determined not by God's standards but by how successful an action is in helping acquire more wealth.

So it is not surprising that Paul added the phrase that "some people, eager for money, have wandered from the faith and pierced themselves with many griefs" (6:10b). They took a wrong turn at a certain point in their lives, and from then on, they traveled along a path that took them farther and farther away from the faith. They were forced into doing so many things that were opposed to the faith that they could no longer hold on to the faith.

The verb "wandered away" is in the passive voice, suggesting that they are helpless and out of control because of their deception. They decided to follow the way of mammon. Now their lives are controlled by the principles of mammon. They have no strength to resist. They are "hooked on" mammon.

Paul's next expression, "and pierced themselves with many griefs" is in the active voice, which shows that they are responsible for their pathetic state. They made the original deliberate choice of mammon over God. Now they are paying the price of it. They sought after wealth at all costs, and now they have it, but they realize the cost was not worth paying. Wealth did not deliver the goods. It only brought disillusionment.

Wealth will never give a lapsed Christian true contentment. A person who has tasted the abundant life of Christ will never be satisfied after it leaves him no matter how much else he gets to put in its place. Christ's life satisfied his deepest yearnings. No amount of money can do that. Now he has condemned himself to remorse and disillusionment.

Paul used some very vivid language in this passage to drive home his point. We are made to realize how serious a sin materialism is. Let us be warned and warn others about its dangers. We have seen that many people get themselves entangled in materialism after taking an initial wrong turn. If we see those under our care at the brink of taking such a turn it is our responsibility as leaders to guide them away from this path.

Now, while we remain alert to the dangers of materialism, we must not forget the beauty of true godliness. Let us be faithful in pointing out, and demonstrating in our lives, that in following God and his ways there is true contentment. And is it not out of a search for contentment that people begin to lust after wealth? They are looking in the wrong place! The yearnings for contentment are ingrained deep down in our beings. An external thing like wealth could not penetrate so deep into us as to satisfy these yearnings. Only God could do that.

PERSONAL APPLICATION

As you look at your life can you say, "I am content with my lot"? If you can, I suggest you pause to praise God for his grace. If you cannot, look for causes for the discontentment and seek to determine how you could eliminate these causes.

FOURTEEN
POSSESSIONS: KEEPING
THE RIGHT ATTITUDE (6:17–19)

The preceding passage was Paul's advice to those aspiring to be rich (6:6-10). Next he gave special advice to those who were already rich (6:17-19). Between these two passages was a digression very typical of Paul. It was a charge to Timothy about some critical areas in Timothy's personal life (6:11-16).

Paul gave what was essentially two commands. The first had to do with the attitudes of the wealthy (6:17) and the second with their actions (6:18, 19).

HUMILITY AND RESPONSIBLE ENJOYMENT (6:17)

Paul urged Timothy to "Command those who are rich in this present world not to be arrogant nor to put their hope in wealth, which is so uncertain, but to put their hope in God" (v. 17a).

The Limited Value of Wealth. Right at the outset, Paul gave a hint about the approach to wealth that he was adopting by describing the wealthy as "those who are rich in this present world." He was alluding to the fact that there was another type of wealth, nobler and more important. Material wealth lasts only for this life, and this life will soon come to an end. So, wealth is a temporary blessing just like physical beauty or musical talent, blessings that are not basic to a fulfilled life. Some people who are not rich in material possessions are very rich from the perspective of eternity, which is what ultimately matters.

We see from this passage that Paul did not demand all wealthy people to renounce their riches completely. But he showed that there was a superior value system according to which material wealth is not considered as being very significant.

Humility and Trusting God. Paul's command about the attitude of the rich had three parts to it. First, they were not to be "arrogant." Wealthy people could mistakenly consider themselves superior to others and thus expect to be treated like special people. The Bible strongly opposes this. James, for example, said we must not reserve the best seats in church for the wealthy (James 2:1-4).

We all know of rich people who have had an unhealthy control over Christian boards and churches. They use their wealth to throw their weight around, demanding obedience, lest they cut off their financial assistance. In a sense, the church was asking for trouble when it appointed such people to positions of responsibility. They were appointed primarily because of their financial and social stature rather than their spiritual stature.

In the kingdom of God, greatness is Christlikeness. And Christlikeness has nothing to do with one's wealth. Christ was a servant Lord, and he said that in his kingdom greatness is measured by servanthood (Matt. 20:25-28), which is the exact opposite of arrogance.

Second, the rich must "not . . . put their hope in wealth which is so uncertain." Some wealthy people may be arrogant because they feel more secure than others due to their prosperity. But wealth is not a good basis for security, for it can be lost in a moment. The writer of Proverbs said, "Cast but a glance at riches, and they are gone, for they will surely sprout wings and fly off to the sky like an eagle" (23:5).

Third, the rich are "to put their trust in God," something the wealthy often find difficult to do. They think they don't need God because they feel sufficient in themselves, not realizing how uncertain their source of security really is.

One who trusts in God has no guarantee that his material wealth is secure. It may suddenly be taken away as Job's was. But Job's loss did not touch the core of his life. The things that ultimately mattered to him had to do with God. And when we, like Job, place our trust in God, we can proclaim with David, amidst all sorts of apparent setbacks, "The Lord will fulfill his purpose for me; your love, O Lord, endures for ever" (Ps. 138:8). This is the confidence one has when he trusts in God. Isaiah wrote, "You will keep in perfect peace him whose mind is steadfast, because he trusts in you" (26:3).

Enjoying God's Provision. Paul continued to underscore the security of hoping in God by saying that God "richly provides us with everything for our enjoyment." As Christians we have access to unlimited wealth, but this verse is not a license for people to amass wealth for themselves. If we want to find out how much we should keep for ourselves and how much we should give to others, there are other Scriptures to consider. What this verse says is that if we follow God, we will have everything that God knows as being good for us, and that what God provides for us is intended to be enjoyed.

The ascetic heretics in Ephesus had been insisting that the truly spiritual must renounce material possessions entirely, a very unbiblical position. According to the biblical doctrine of creation, God made this world good, which means its material resources are also good. If they are used responsibly according to God's purposes, they can be legitimately enjoyed. The word used for enjoyment here is a strong word. The Christian has been gifted with joy by God. And part of this Christian joy is experienced when Christians use material things in a responsible way.

Responsible Christian enjoyment cannot be extravagant or selfish. We certainly may need a change from the normal routine of eating at home, but we don't need to go to the most expensive restaurant in town. We like to go to a plush restaurant because it makes us feel good and gives us a new sense of importance. Money that could have been given to the spiritually and economically deprived is being wasted in boosting a flagging ego that is looking for recognition from empty status—a status which has nothing to do with the heart of Christianity.

The principle of unnecessary extravagance also applies to such events as the wedding celebrations and dinner parties people host. Often large sums of money are spent on these occasions simply because of the status value attached to such expenditure.

How important it is for Christians to learn to enjoy themselves inexpensively without regarding that enjoyment as cheap! In the kingdom it is empty status that is cheap—not simple beauty.

There are ample opportunities for wholesome and simple beauty and enjoyment available to Christians which give much greater fulfillment and fun than a lot of these extravagant status symbols.

One more point needs to be made about enjoyment. The Christian's enjoyment is always within the limits of Christian love. A Christian may suddenly be faced with an urgent need to which the principle of love beckons him to respond. But the only money he may have is what had been reserved for some enjoyment, such as a vacation or a special meal. If he senses that God wants him to give this money, he will do so and forego the enjoyment. Yet this is no great sacrifice, for God in turn will provide us with all the joy we need to more than compensate for the "sacrifice" we made. God provides for us richly for our enjoyment. But love is our primary aim in life—not enjoyment (1 Cor. 14:1).

GENEROSITY (6:18)

After a command about the attitudes of the wealthy, Paul gave instructions about their actions: "Command them to do good, to be rich in good deeds, and to be generous and willing to share" (6:18). This command too is in three parts.

Good Deeds. The first requirement of the rich is to "do good and to be rich in good deeds." Earlier Paul described one type of riches—material possessions, reducing their value by adding to "rich" the words "in this present world." Next he gave a more valuable type of riches—good deeds, a favorite topic of the Pastoral Epistles. Good deeds are required of all church members (Titus 2:14; 3:8, 14), of Christian women (1 Tim. 2:10; 5:10), of leaders (Titus 2:7), and here, of rich people. These deeds often take the form of little things done to people to bring joy to them or to lighten their load.

Giving and receiving such kindnesses are an important part of a healthy and complete life. Yet people often think that such acts of kindness have no place in the lives of leaders and rich people. They have too many lofty duties and responsibilities that, they believe, release them from such mundane activities. Sometimes these so-called insignificant deeds are despised by people who are aspiring toward "lofty" goals.

I remember with regret a sermon given at an evangelistic rally in Sri Lanka by a preacher from a foreign land. He said that a commitment to Christ had nothing to do with such actions as helping little old ladies across the street. He made this statement many times in a very derogatory manner. I kept wishing that the Buddhists and Hindus in the audience would not take offense at that statement and thus be detracted from the gospel. Such actions are given a high place in their religions. And it should be so in Christianity also—not as a means of attaining merit, but as expressions of obedience to our servant Lord.

Before Paul asked the rich to give, he told them to be rich in good deeds. It is not enough for them to dole out funds in a detached way. They must become involved with deeds of kindness. It will help others and also help them to live complete lives.

Generosity. Next Paul said that the rich are "to be generous." Some people lavish themselves with good things, but Christians are to be lavish in the way they give to others.

The Christian's motivation for generosity is many-sided: (1) He has as his example Jesus Christ, who though he was rich yet for our sakes became poor (2 Cor. 8:9); (2) He has a love in his heart that constrains—compels—him to share what he has with others (2 Cor. 5:14); (3) He is surrounded by a world ridden with glaring inequality—a world originally made good by God, but ruined because man did not carry out his responsibility to manage it properly. Paul explained how the desire for equality motivates Christian giving (2 Cor. 8:13). I believe we are far too quick to dismiss as irrelevant the words of John the Baptist explaining what it meant to produce "fruit in keeping with repentance" (Luke 3:8). John said, "The man with two tunics should share with him who has none and the one who has food should do the same" (Luke 3:11).

In the world today ten thousand people die of starvation every day and many more, without a knowledge of the gospel of Christ. How important then is the call to generosity in today's society! The historic Lausanne Covenant sought to come to grips with the implications of living in a hungry world when it declared: "Those of us who live in affluent circumstances accept our duty to develop a simple life-style in order to contribute more generously to both relief and evangelism." If we make generosity a personal ambition, an inevitable result would be a simpler life-style.

Sadly, however, as people get richer, their catalogue of "essentials" for living also usually becomes much larger. New "legitimate" expenses appear in the budget. What was once a luxury has now become a necessity. These people have a new status in society. They have started to compare themselves with a new set of people. And they develop a new style of life in keeping with their new status.

The media are also of no help in this area. As Ron Sider puts it, "Advertising constantly convinces us that we really need one unnecessary luxury after another. The standard of living is the god of twentieth-century America, and the ad man is its prophet" (*The Graduated Tithe,* InterVarsity, 1978). What Sider says of America is alas becoming increasingly true of other societies around the world.

Many people think they cannot "afford" to be generous. When you ask them why they do not give, they say they have no money. That is true, for they have too many new expenses!

One's style of life is decided by how one decides he is going to spend his money. The Christian must always give high priority to giving when deciding on expenditures. Most people choose a style of life that involves so much expenditure for other things that there is hardly anything left for giving. They give only from their excess—that is, if there is an excess! The true Christian considers giving when deciding on how he will spend his money, not after deciding. Giving such priority to generosity in our lives is a discipline to cultivate, especially because it is so easy to convince ourselves that we must spend so much on personal necessities resulting in our having nothing left for giving.

The Bible has many surprisingly harsh warnings to wealthy people. We often dismiss the story of the rich young ruler by saying that wealth was the problem of that particular man, but not a problem to everybody. Yet at the end of this story, after the disappointed young man leaves the presence of Christ, Jesus said it would be hard for any rich man to enter the kingdom. Of course, he did go on to say that what is impossible with man is possible with God. But that does not reduce the force of Christ's warning. As far as we know, that rich young man was never saved. This story teaches us, as Peter Davids has pointed out, that "wealth is one of the greatest barriers to [total] commitment, perhaps the greatest" *(Living More Simply,* InterVarsity, 1980).

How can a person find out how much he should keep for himself and how much he should give and where to draw the line between necessities and luxuries? Let me suggest a few guidelines:

1. He needs to make this decision prayerfully, taking seriously what the Bible teaches about the use and abuse of money.

2. He should share this with others who are close to him in the Christian community and his own family members. Their objective advice will be a great help. They will, for example, help him avoid making rash decisions about spending or about giving. They may be able to see through his excuses and rationalizations. Personal finances, however, is an area which most people are reluctant to discuss freely with others. Even some who are strongly committed to community life prefer to keep the area of personal finances to themselves.

3. God will most surely speak to a person who sincerely desires to find out his will about how to use personal wealth. He must wait for God's guidance without making rash decisions.

4. And when God shows the way to go, let him walk along it, whatever the cost.

Willingness to Share. The last part of Paul's second command to the rich is a call to be "willing to share." The Greek word translated "share" *(koinonikos)* comes from the word for fellowship *(koinonia).* It places the emphasis upon the relationship the giver should have with those who receive. Paul reminded us that the generous Macedonians, who gave to the church in Jerusalem, first gave themselves (2 Cor. 8:1-5). True Christian love demands both, and giving money is no substitute for the giving of ourselves.

Many relevant implications can be drawn from this call to share oneself when giving. It has something to say about the relationship between Christian donor organizations and those who receive their aid. On the one hand, the donor should not dictate terms to the receivers and treat them as inferior people. On the other hand, the donor should not completely release himself from any responsibility toward the receiver after giving the assistance. I believe the answer to this lies in the idea of sharing. What is needed is a spiritual relationship between the donor and the receiver. They have been brought together in a unique relationship involving the stewardship of God's (not the donor's) money. The donor is the channel through which God makes the money available to the receiver. The receiver is to use this money for God's glory.

As in all proper relationships, here too there are responsibilities and obligations, especially when money or other material resources are involved. Mutually acceptable guidelines may have to be set up to help keep the relationship healthy. But always the basis of this relationship is a spiritual comradeship coming out of the idea of sharing.

Another implication of sharing is the donor's identification with those who receive his gifts. If God calls us to give to the poor, we must also be willing to identify with them. Otherwise, there will be no sharing. This identification may place on us some obligations which are even more demanding than those associated with material giving. When we seek to relieve the hardship of the poor with our gifts, God may call us to seek solutions to a deeper problem—the cause for that hardship. We may have to deal with questions such as whether or not these people are poor because they do not have reasonable opportunities for advancement. Are these people receiving all the benefits that are constitutionally their right? Is there an injustice in the system which automatically results in discrimination against them? Do these people know the Savior in whom alone lies the answer to their deepest needs? These questions deal with causes for spiritual and economic poverty. And sharing with the poor must involve an effort to alleviate these causes of poverty.

Identification often causes us to reexamine our life-style. How can we properly identify with people who have nothing when we waste what we have through extravagant expenditure? The poor will never understand such extravagance and it would become a barrier to a meaningful relationship—a barrier that must be removed if true fellowship is to be established.

Sharing can be a demanding activity. Because it is, many prefer to give to the poor but at a safe distance. For example, an urban Christian may try to identify with a group of rural poor people through gifts and occasional visits. During these visits he will try to live as they live. But he comes back home and lives a completely different life. Now there are poor slum dwellers a few yards from his home. He sees them every day, but he makes no attempt to identify with them. He builds a high wall around himself and his family (sometimes literally!) so as to insulate himself from these "dangerous elements." Any attempt to identify with them would involve a threat to his present comfortable life-style which is too unsettling to handle. So he soothes his conscience by temporarily identifying with the poor who are far from home.

The issue of motives and attitudes in giving has often surfaced in this discussion. We have presented some good and bad motives and attitudes associated with giving. This discussion would not be complete if I do not mention two more unchristian motives in giving.

Some give with a desire for self-acclaim. When they decide on where to give their money, they incline toward those causes which would more effectively make the public know about the gift. Churches and Christian organizations have often played into Satan's trap in this area. They make it known that gifts given to them will be publicly recognized. They proclaim directly or indirectly, "Give, and have your name appear in our magazine," or "Give, and have a plaque put up with your name on it." Such gifts have little spiritual power behind them. The donor through his gift becomes a partner in the ministry which receives the gift. But because of his spiritual barrenness, the ministry of which he is now a part also gets tainted with barrenness.

The programs sponsored in this way may prosper and show tangible results. Our methods of measuring success are usually directly related to the bigness of a program. With a lot of money one can have a very big program. Impressive statistics can be shown. But on the last day, when the fires of God's judgment are applied to these programs, it will be revealed that they also were built on wood, hay, and straw.

Another type of giving arising out of wrong motives is reminiscent of what in past centuries was called the buying of indulgences. Some people have gotten rich or are maintaining their wealth by unchristian means. They exploit the poor. They underpay their workers. They are dishonest. They brutally cut down competitors. These people, of course, will be troubled by an uneasy conscience, especially if they come from a religious background. Their giving may be an effort to compensate for their continuing injustices and to soothe a troubled conscience. These types of giving are alien to the spirit of generosity and sharing advocated by Paul.

TREASURES IN HEAVEN (6:19)

A Wise Investment. Paul described the rewards of Christian generosity: "In this way they will lay up treasure for themselves as a firm foundation for the coming age, so that they may take hold of the life that is truly life" (v. 19). The generous not only help others. They are actually helping themselves in the process of giving. The stress in this sentence is on "themselves."

Every gift given in a Christian way is a wise investment in what John Wesley called, "the bank of heaven." To substantiate this Wesley cited Proverbs 19:17: "He who is kind to the poor lends to the Lord, and he will reward him for what he has done" and Matthew 25:40: "I tell you the truth, whatever you did for one of the least of these brothers of mine, you did it for me." These verses point out that when we give to the poor we are in reality giving to God. So Wesley said, "Give to the poor with a single eye, with an upright heart, and write, 'so much given to God' " *(Forty-Four Sermons,* London: Epworth Press, 1967).

In the Sermon on the Mount, Jesus talked about those who "have received their reward in full" on earth (Matt. 6:2, 5, 16). A little later, Jesus said that the Christian's reward is in heaven (Matt. 6:19-21). The focus in this passage, and in Paul's statement in 1 Timothy 6:19, is on the wisdom of using possessions according to God's principles. People who give in an unchristian way may receive an immediate reward on earth. But this reward expends itself completely on earth. Not so with service rendered in God's way. So the right kind of giving is a wise investment.

When a wise person receives some money, he asks the question, "How am I going to achieve the most with this money?" He may decide to put it in a fixed deposit in a bank or a finance company and earn some interest from it. Or he may decide to invest in a business enterprise, or build a house, or buy some furniture. However, the Bible teaches that the most permanent investment is the investment made in heaven. It is put to use in the work of the Kingdom of God. Because this kingdom is an eternal one, the fruit of our work will also last for eternity. The words "firm foundation" which Paul used focus on the security of this investment.

Very rarely do people regard giving as an investment. They think of it as a duty or as a sacrifice made at the cost of something else that could have been done with the money. They don't think of giving as putting their money to work in a development scheme which grows and grows until it enters the sphere of eternity. But this is what Christian giving is!

Paul concluded this verse by saying that the Christian who gives takes "hold of the life that is truly life." People who live for themselves never get the security and fulfillment they pursue. Wealth cannot satisfy the deepest needs of man. A man may be rich on the outside but a pauper inside. The one who trusts and obeys Christ has an abundant life in this world (John 10:10). And we know that this life coming through the Holy Spirit who was indwelt us is but a foretaste of a much more abundant life that awaits us in the next world (2 Cor. 1:22; 5:5; Eph. 1:14).

Is Heavenly Reward a Selfish Motive for Service? When Paul and Jesus talked about rewards in heaven, were they appealing to man's selfish desires? Do we do good only because we are to be rewarded in heaven? I believe the words about rewards in heaven are given as an encouragement to faith, as an assurance of the wisdom of kingdom living amidst constant bombardment from outside that what we are doing is folly.

No one likes to appear foolish in front of others. Helping the truly needy usually has no status value on earth. The truly needy are so powerless that their gratitude rarely makes an impact on society. So people don't know how much you have helped the powerless. Besides, the Christian operates from the resolve not to let the left hand know what the right hand is doing (Matt. 6:3). So, real Christian generosity rarely gets press coverage and rarely enhances progress in society.

Then there is the humiliation of being "taken for a ride" which sooner or later will happen, however careful one is. Other people usually delight in talking about such humiliation.

Then there is the fact that often the sacrificial gifts of a relatively wealthy Christian are rarely appreciated by others. They think he is giving out of his excess. "He has so much," they say, "that is nothing for him." Because he does not publicize his giving, they don't know that he has given similar gifts to numerous other people. What was to him a sacrifice was regarded by others to be crumbs from his table, which is what a lot of giving is today. The genuinely generous Christian is also lumped with everybody else, a fact which makes a truly generous rich Christian a lonely figure.

Is all this humiliation and loneliness worthwhile? This is a question with which many people struggle. Because of this price, many opt to drop out of the Christian way and instead choose to follow an easier way. They may still give to Christian activity. But they don't give according to truly Christian principles, which to them have become too costly to follow. To the faithful who struggle with loneliness and with having to appear to be foolish, Jesus and Paul offered words of encouragement by pointing to a heavenly reward. It is not folly—it is the wisest investment one could make.

The word "command" appears twice in this passage. It shows that if Timothy was to lead the Christians in Ephesus faithfully, he would have to instruct them carefully about the Christian attitude toward possessions. Today we find so many Christians who are not effective in Christian service or who have even completely betrayed the faith due to being choked by the deceitfulness of wealth (Matt. 13:22). Yet today it is very rarely that we hear preaching and teaching on the topic of possessions. How important then it is for leaders to start carefully instructing Christians about the biblical attitude to wealth!

PERSONAL APPLICATION

Every Christian should develop a personal philosophy and plan of giving. Write your plan or proposed plan in about three or four sentences.

CONCLUSION

A new Christian periodical from Canada, *Faith Alive,* chose the
topic of leadership as the main emphasis for its inaugural issue
(Faith Alive, I, 1, 1983). Its opening article by Brian Stiller was
entitled "Leaders: A Vanishing Breed?" This and other articles
asserted that there was a crisis of leadership in the church in
Canada. Neil Snider spoke of "a dearth of leadership" and observed that "young people who should be emerging into major
leadership roles are not" ("Leadership in Crisis?" pp. 14, 15).

This crisis is not confined to Canada. The Asian church struggles
with the same problem. And I believe this is a problem in other
continents too. This book is a modest attempt to contribute to the
raising up of a new generation of Christian leaders.

Snider has said that one of the issues related to the leadership
crisis is the "anti-leader bias that presently dominates much of our
society's thinking." Partly responsible for this bias is the fact that
"we are afraid of the strong man leader. We've seen leaders go
bad." So, people don't want to trust strong leaders. Snider says
that because of this mistrust, "If one ever should emerge as a
leader in our Christian circles we make sure to pull him down in a
hurry so he can't do anything."

I believe one of the great needs in the church today is for a new
crop of leaders who, by their exemplary lives, will help restore in
people's minds the esteem which the work of leadership deserves

to have. So I do not apologize for devoting so much space in this book to discussing the character and example of a leader. In fact, this could be considered the key emphasis of this book.

Another contributing factor to the crisis in leadership is what Brian Stiller describes as a new style of leadership that has emerged in the church. Our leaders today are essentially managers, says Stiller. We have developed and established our Christian structures which now need people who will help keep them running smoothly. As Stiller says, "Movements need leaders to point out direction whereas empires require planners."

We have described the leader not as a manager but as a parent, a discipler, or a guru. This is the second key emphasis of this book. A leader's relationship with those he leads is essentially one of love. As love is the most important feature of Christian behavior, it is essential that love invade the core of Christian leadership too. The parent-discipler-guru method of leadership allows love to do that.

The loving aim of a Christian leader is to lead the people of God and the organization to which they belong to a full realization of God's will for them. He seeks to take God's people forward, holding their hand, as it were, into new exploits for God. In order to do this properly, he cares for the flock and ensures that their needs are met. He teaches the flock. He encourages and rebukes them. He equips them so that they can use their gifts to the fullest. He motivates them to keep fighting the battles of the kingdom, and to keep on advancing into new territories of conquest. As he fulfills these roles the whole body, along with him, moves forward to experience the inexhaustible possibilities contained within the will of God.

It is my prayer that this book will help its readers traverse this path to biblical leadership; that they will place uppermost in their aspirations the dual calling to be models and to be spiritual parents.

BIBLIOGRAPHY

Barclay, William. *The Daily Study Bible: The Letters to Timothy, Titus, and Philemon.* Philadelphia: Westminster Press, 1960.

_____ . *New Testament Words.* Philadelphia: Westminster Press, 1974.

Barrett, Ethel. *Will the Real Phony Please Stand Up.* Glendale: Regal, 1969.

Boreham, F. W. *Daily Readings from F. W. Boreham.* Edited by Frank Cumbers. London: Hodder and Stoughton, 1976.

Bubna, Donald L. *Building People through a Caring Sharing Fellowship.* Wheaton, IL: Tyndale House, 1978.

Coleman, Robert E. *The Master Plan of Evangelism.* Old Tappan, NJ: Revell, 1964.

Davids, Peter. *Living More Simply.* Edited by Ronald J. Sider. Downers Grove, IL: InterVarsity, 1980.

Demaray, Donald E. *Preacher Aflame!* Grand Rapids, MI: Baker, 1972.

Eims, Leroy. *The Lost Art of Disciple Making.* Grand Rapids, MI: Zondervan, 1978.

Guthrie, Donald. *The Pastoral Epistles.* London: Tyndale Press, 1959.

Harrison, Everett. *Acts: The Expanding Church.* Chicago: Moody Press, 1975.

Hendrichsen, Walter. *Disciples Are Made—Not Born.* Wheaton, IL: Victor Books, 1974.

Hendriksen, William. *The New Testament Commentary, I & II Timothy and Titus.* Edinburgh: The Banner of Truth Trust, 1960.

Hiebert, D. Edmond. *First Timothy, Everyman's Bible Commentary.* Chicago: Moody Press, 1957.

Hughes, Philip. *Creative Minds in Contemporary Theology,* Grand Rapids: Eerdmans, 1969.

Jones, E. Stanley. *The Word Became Flesh.* Nashville: Abingdon, 1963.

Kelly, J. N. D. *A Commentary on the Pastoral Epistles.* London: Adams & Charles Black, 1963.

Lloyd-Jones, Martyn. *Preaching and Preachers.* Grand Rapids, MI: Zondervan, 1972.

Mains, Karen Burton. *Open Heart—Open Home.* Elgin, IL: David C. Cook, 1976.

Martin, Ralph P. *Colossians and Philemon, New Century Bible Commentary.* Grand Rapids, MI: Eerdmans, 1973.

_____ . *Worship in the Early Church.* London: Morgan and Scott, 1972.

McCheyne, Robert Murray. *Bible Reading Calendar.* Edinburgh: The Banner of Truth Trust, n.d.

Miller, Basil. *George Mueller: Man of Faith.* Minneapolis: Bethany, 1972.

Palms, Roger. *Upon a Penny Loaf: The Wisdom of John Bunyan.* Minneapolis: Bethany, 1978.

Parker, Mrs. Arthur. *Sadhu Sundar Singh: Called of God.* Madras: The Christian Literature Society, 1918.

Sanders, J. Oswald. *Spiritual Leadership.* London: Lakeland, 1967.

Sangster, W. E. *The Approach to Preaching.* Grand Rapids, MI: Baker, 1974. Reprint.

_____ . *Power in Preaching.* Grand Rapids, MI: Baker, 1976. Reprint.

_____ . *A Spiritual Check-up.* London: Epworth Press, 1976. Reprint.

Seamands, John T. *Tell It Well: Communicating the Gospel Across Cultures.* Kansas City: Beacon Hill Press, 1981.

Scott, E. F. *The Pastoral Epistles.* London: Hodder and Stoughton, 1936.

Sider, Ronald J. *The Graduated Tithe.* Downers Grove, IL: InterVarsity, 1978.

Stott, John R. W. *Guard the Gospel.* Downers Grove, IL: InterVarsity, 1973.

_____ . *I Believe in Preaching.* London: Hodder and Stoughton, 1982.

_____ . *The Preacher's Portrait.* London: The Tyndale Press, 1961.

Torrey, R. A. *Personal Work.* Old Tappan, NJ: Revell, n.d.

Towns, Elmer. *The Christian Hall of Fame.* Grand Rapids: Baker, 1971.

Trench, Richard C. *Synonyms of the New Testament.* Grand Rapids: Eerdmans, 1973. Reprint of 1880 edition.

Wesley, John. *Forty-four Sermons.* London: Epworth Press, 1967. Reprint of 1787 edition.

Wiersbe, Warren W. *Listening to the Giants.* Grand Rapids, MI: Baker, 1980.

Zondervan Pictorial Encyclopedia of the Bible. Edited by Merrill C. Tenney. Grand Rapids, MI: Zondervan, 1975.

PERIODICALS

Bayly, Joseph. "The How-to Church." *Eternity,* Jan. 1983, p. 15.
Snider, Neil. "Leadership in Crisis?" *Faith Alive,* I, 1, 1983.
Stiller, Brian. "Leaders: A Vanishing Breed?" *Faith Alive,* I, 1, 1983.

How Come It's Taking Me So Long?, Lane Adams. A book to help new and growing Christians to understand the process of Christian growth. Thirteen sessions.

How to Get What You Pray For, Dr. Bill Austin. A study of how Christians can achieve greater success in prayer once they learn how to put themselves in harmony with the essential agents of prayer. Thirteen sessions.

How to Help a Friend, Paul Welter. A study designed to teach Christians how to discover a friend's "living channels," and tips on expressing warmth, identifying needs, and responding to crises. Thirteen sessions.

How to Really Know the Will of God, Richard Strauss. Practical suggestions for decision making discovered in God's Word. Thirteen sessions.

Leadership Life-style, Ajith Fernando. A clear examination of leadership training found in Paul's letters to Timothy. Thirteen sessions.

Listen! Jesus Is Praying, Warren W. Wiersbe. A verse-by-verse commentary on Christ's High Priestly Prayer in John 17 with practical applications. Thirteen sessions.

Live Up to Your Faith: Studies in Titus, James T. Draper, Jr. Christianity is more than right doctrines. Paul's message concerned both right believing and right living. Thirteen sessions.

Man Overboard, Sinclair B. Ferguson. A study of the life of Jonah. Not a story of a great fish but of a great God who deals with those who struggle with obedience. Six sessions.

Marriage Is for Love, Dr. Richard Strauss. An insightful look at God's principles of happy marriage. A study to strengthen the fabric of your marriage. Thirteen sessions.

Parents, Take Charge! Perry L. Draper. A psychologist explains important principles on child-rearing found in God's Word. Thirteen sessions.

Passport to the Bible, Bobi Hromas. Five minutes a day of Bible study and the Word comes alive. Bible study methods and dozens of ways to read, understand, and apply Bible truth. Thirteen sessions.

Proverbs: Practical Directions for Living, James T. Draper, Jr. A book to help people get a handle on studying Proverbs. Thirteen sessions.

Reality of Hell and the Goodness of God, The, Harold T. Bryson. A study of the biblical doctrine of hell and how it is consistent with a good and gracious God. Six sessions.

Run with the Winners, Warren W. Wiersbe. A study of Hebrews 11 and the "Hall of Fame of Faith." Defines biblical faith and how it works. Thirteen sessions.

Self-Control, Russell Kelfer. A study of the enemies of self-control—the attitudes, appetites, and activities that threaten to control our lives. Thirteen sessions.

Sex Roles and the Christian Family, W. Peter Blitchington. There is a specific pattern for family relationships designed by God and set in motion for our benefit. Thirteen sessions.

Spirit-Controlled Temperament, Dr. Tim LaHaye. A guide to understanding your God-given personality strengths and what the Holy Spirit can do to overcome your weaknesses. Thirteen sessions.

Standing on the Rock: The Importance of Biblical Inerrancy, James Montgomery Boice. A study outlining the current controversy and the importance of accepting the Bible as inerrant. Six sessions.

Ten Commandments, The, J. I. Packer. God in love gave us not only the gospel but the law. A study of God's moral absolutes. Six sessions.

What the Faith Is All About, Elmer L. Towns. A layman's approach to Bible doctrine that provides the solid content for the development of believers. Fifty-two sessions.

What To Do Till the Lord Comes: Studies in 1 & 2 Thessalonians, Dr. James T. Draper, Jr. A relevant message to the church trying to remain faithful amidst opposition. Thirteen sessions.